Strange Realities
true stories about the hardly believable

This is the sixth book by **L. Mason Jones** to be published by Arena Books. The Author served a number of years in the military, and travelling on a so-called 'government service' passport, found himself in such places as south Yemen, Bahrain, the Gulf of Oman, Cyprus and Germany. After leaving the service, he became part of the team producing the highly successful business jet, The Hawker 125. He functioned as a quality-engineering inspector with, initially, British Aerospace then Corporate Jets Inc and finally Raytheon USA, the latter of which purchased the thriving business and moved production to the USA. Mr Jones then left the business to concentrate on writing projects. He has three adult offspring and resides in Chester.

By the same Author –

Monkey Trial 2000
Pillars of Fire
When The Moon Came Cultural Shock
The Human Enigma

Strange Realities

True stories about the hardly believable

L. Mason Jones

Arena Books

Copyright © L. Mason Jones 2021

The right of L. Mason Jones to be identified as author of this work has been asserted in accordance with the Copyright, Designs and Patents Act 1988.

First published by Arena Books in 2021

Arena Books
6 Southgate Green
Bury St. Edmunds
IP33 2BL.

www.arenabooks.co.uk

All rights reserved. Except for the quotation of short passages for the purposes of criticism and review, no part of this publication may be reproduced, stored in a retrieval system, or transmitted, in any form or by any means, electronic, mechanical, photocopying, recording or otherwise, without the prior permission of the publisher.

L. Mason Jones
Strange Realities *true stories of the hardly believable*

British Library cataloguing in Publication Data. A Catalogue record for this book is available from the British Library.

ISBN 978-1-914390-04-3

BIC categories:- PDA, PGK, RBC, RBGD, PDZ, ABGF, PGS, RNR, TTD.

Printed & bound by Lightning Source UK

Cover design
by Jason Anscomb

Typeset in
Times New Roman

CONTENTS

CHAPTER I	The Count of St. Germain	Page 9
CHAPTER II	Am I Really Dead ?	Page 36
CHAPTER III	Sunk but not Forgotten	Page 68
CHAPTER IV	I Cimbed on Noah's Ark	Page 83
CHAPTER V	All Those Noah's	Page 93
CHAPTER VI	My Carbon Footprint	Page 117

***

CHAPTER I

THE COUNT ST GERMAIN

You can do your best by researching, analysing, studying and trawling through many pages of literature but it is doubtful that you will ever encounter another person that would be comparable to the amazing, charismatic, enigmatic character that we will be dealing with in this chapter.

I refer to the incomparable Count St. Germain, surely one of the most unbelievable men that have ever appeared in history. So much so, that one might almost write off the amazing story of, and the many things he achieved in his extraordinary long lifespan as little more than fiction or that, it was simply a hoax, but this is not possible.

One has to believe in him and the things he achieved, simply because so many other people, who were known to have existed in history were alive during the lifetime of the Count and where contemporaneous with him. They knew him, conferred with him and were often amazed regarding the things that they knew he could accomplish.

St. Germain was an alchemist, could turn base metals into gold and silver. He discovered the elixir of youth. He was a philosopher, composer, a violinist and a linguist. He could manufacture diamonds, remove flaws from diamonds and could manufacture high quality pearls with a fine lustre.

The aforementioned people who knew St. Germain, where nobility, lords, ladies and eminent people of history, such as King Louis XV no less and other lesser dignitaries. Because of all these people the existence and the accomplishments of St. Germain cannot be denied as they are documented in history and in the memoirs of so many people that were so impressed by his deeds, they felt they had to write of him in their (what could be called) diaries.

His many exploits, within the social circles in which he moved, are as said, well documented as are personages he rubbed shoulders with. They include royalty and nobility, not only of France but many other countries throughout the world during his seemingly endless existence.

He seemed to be blessed with enormous longevity yet his life, in parts, is shrouded in clouds of mystery. At this point, it would be appropriate, I feel, to be able to quote precisely when this enigmatic individual was born and also when he died (if indeed he ever did). This remark in brackets may seem poignant but as you read on, you will soon realise the significance of it.

We cannot be exact about some aspects of the Count's life, as he popped up in various countries of Europe at (and affecting) significant events in those countries historic records.

With regard to the birth of Count St Germain, some accounts have suggested that he was born in the 1600's and a certain Annie Bessant, who co- authored a book titled *The Compte De St. Germain*. 'The Secret of Kings' stated that he was born the son of Francis Racoczi II, the Prince of Transylvania in 1690. Other versions stretch his lifetime back enormously. Even though, as we have said, his existence cannot be denied, this does not mean that everything we do read about the Count is factual, unless supported by notable people who were present.

The old account on which the above factors are based may seem to stray into the realms of fantasy, which sometimes happens during the usual process of embellishing a good story. If the Count was born in 1690, he was still very much in his prime a hundred years later.

However, for all that, it will become clear that the incredible Count was seemingly quite 'upfront' and open with regard to his abilities as an accomplished alchemist. As a matter of fact, he was said to be a grand master of this ancient and mysterious art form.

To be able to transform base metals into gold and silver is known as transmutation and it will be shown that the Count's abilities in this regard are not just based on hearsay; he did it, as will be shown, for an acquaintance before his eyes. When we read of the historical alchemists such as Paracelsus for example, we tend to formulate in our minds a bearded mysterious looking figure in a gloomy room full of glassware, beavering away in this strange laboratory to the sound of hubbly bubbly simmering and steam emanating from glass retorts, with all the various ingredients being marinated together. However, with regard to St. Germain, the impression is given of more knowledgeable and far more successful work, producing more positive results being seen to be achieved. Nevertheless, when we look closely at the work of St. Germain, he appeared to make it all seem quite easy.

If his gold and silver producing was not enough, he was said to be able to 'manufacture' flawless diamonds an accomplishment that certainly stretches ones imagination or belief, especially when we consider the quite enormous pressures along with the other scientific processes required, in particular the equipment to produce the very high temperatures required to produce even basic industrial diamonds, let alone large flawless items. In fact diamonds of any size, as the Count was said to be able to accomplish he would have had to reproduce the major forces that exist within the Earth, in some kind of specially equipped scientific laboratory.

It would seem much easier at this point to take the easy path and simply write it all off as pure fantasy or nonsense but as this account will show, we must proceed with caution. In order to achieve all this, he would need enormous wealth he had it. He would need large and private premises he got it. He would need a rich and powerful mentor; he got it in the form of the French King who also afforded him the protection he needed.

We have said that the Count moved in the highest circles. He could not get much higher than the courtly figure that included King Louis XV of France.

The Count was a good friend of Louis and had lengthy discourse with him, with long conversations regarding his alchemical abilities and no doubt, the specialist equipment required to produce the goods.

His friendship with the King came to fruition after he was introduced to the King around 1749 due to the actions of a certain 'Marshal De Belle Isle' and Madame de Pompadour, who was mistress to the King. It will be shown that both the 'Madame' and the King had a vested interest in nurturing this friendship for their own ends with regard to the alleged abilities that were now circulating in Royal Circles regarding the mysterious St. Germain.

Just as those who, when first becoming enlightened regarding the said achievements of the Count, are initially rather sceptical, so indeed was the King initially and not immediately impressed by the courtly gossip who 'knew a friend, that knew someone' etc. He would make it his business to find out for himself.

As time went by, the King decided that he would embrace any possibility that may help to increase his stock of jewels and diamonds and naturally, of course, the gold, silver and even high quality pearls that this valuable friend was said to be able to produce so easily. The King's initial scepticism quickly came to an end when he observed St Germain's own diamonds.

The King was particularly overawed when he saw how flawless St Germain's diamonds were and also, that they seemed far more larger and more pure than his own.

It must be said that in his time (the King) the stories and alleged achievements of the alchemists were more prevalent at that time than in latter centuries. The King had made himself fully conversant with references to the philosopher's stone and more particularly the so-called 'elixir of eternal youth'.

This was of particular interest and much sought after by the ladies of the court and the nobility and in this regard were drawn to the life and alleged achievements of the Count who was also said to be very proficient in the manufacture of effective cosmetics.

The ladies 'vied and jockeyed' into position to obtain an advantage in this regard and to gain favour and attention with the Count. Some made it quite clear that they would 'do anything'. In addition, they would be prepared to go to any expense to obtain the most important item, the elixir of youth and of course the cosmetics rumoured to restore a youthful appearance.

King Louis was more orientated toward the secrets of the alchemical process in order to produce gold, soon he made it clear to St Germain that if he would impart the 'recipe' as he called it, he would want for nothing and that he would be handsomely rewarded 'gratis', with a mansion and a pension (and no doubt a substantial sum of money).

If the Count had been of an entirely mercenary nature, there is little doubt that he would have immediately accepted this generous offer. However, it became clear at that point just how strong was the character and personality of St Germain and how he valued his own abilities. Instead of 'bowing the knee' to the King in gratitude, this did not happen.

The King must have been somewhat taken aback when St Germain displayed this unimpressionable and rather 'cool' attitude. St Germain made it clear to the King that he had no need of such things and to make his point, he immediately took out a handful of diamonds from his coat pocket, almost as though it was merely a handful of loose change given in a lavish tip.

He strew the diamonds out onto a round table in front of the King and simply explained that they where a gift to the King. One could imagine the 'sharp intake of breath' that would have occurred among the Royal audience at this unexpected reaction.

St Germain, not wishing to display any disrespect or disdain, regarding the King's generous offer, he quickly explained that the diamonds where not 'bought' items, but had in fact been manufactured by the Count himself and are the result of his own abilities and art.

Any thoughts that the King and his courtly attendants may have had that the Count may be a charlatan or hoaxer where quickly dispelled.

The King immediately made his mind up that he was not going to let go of this 'goose that could produce all his golden eggs', jewels and pearls included and was quite determined to further this friendship to his maximum advantage, perhaps not realising (or caring) that he was also falling in nicely with St Germain's own plans.

STRANGE REALITIES

So it came to pass that St Germain was provided with a magnificent chateau to occupy and further his arts in peace. This was 'engineered' by the King in order that he could involve himself in the secret work of St Germain and that he would be happy to be an 'apprentice' in the learning mode, to the Count.

This arrangement suited the Count equally for the facilities required for his art, the privacy and the Royal Patronage all fell in with his plans as the Count had become the subject of envy unwanted attention and adverse publicity as it will be shown.

Nevertheless, the King, as said, made it clear to ST Germain that he wished to study under his tutelage in order to learn all the finer points of his ancient art himself. Of course, St Germain made the King well aware of the lifetimes that had been spent by others in pursuit of these arts and that the King could not expect to be able to gather all this knowledge in a few weeks.

In order to highlight how much he must have impressed the notables of his day, we must refer to the strange and often favourable comments directed toward St Germain in his lifetime from people who crossed his path during his travels and very long lifetime.

They were people who were known to have existed in his lifetime. Voltaire for example said of St Germain, "He is a man who knows everything, and who never dies". In stark contrast to that comment, there were others that did not seem to be quite complimentary and as will be shown, quite contradictory.

During his other more extensive travels, he also made more 'closer to home', visits, for example when he appeared in England in 1745, the known historical figure, Horace Walpole, said of St Germain "He sings, plays the violin wonderfully, composes music and is quite mad and not very sensible". This is quite obviously a very strange comment to make, not only in terms of its contradictory nature (when contemplating on the comment by Voltaire) but Louis XV and other French dignitaries.

It is also contradictory within a single sentence, by that we mean, that half of the sentence is positive in the early part but clearly negative and disdainful in the second half. If he impressed Walpole so much with his comments about his musical talents and composing abilities then it does not make any sense to refer to him as 'mad and not very sensible'.

There is however, a possible explanation for this anomaly, which will make sense later on, when it is realised the amazing things that he involved himself in when in countries besides Europe and over such long time periods as to seem almost unbelievable. Yet once again, historic and actual personages vouch for them indirectly in their memoirs.

If he casually mentioned them to Walpole in a matter of fact way, then Walpole may be forgiven for assuming St Germain was delusory or 'quite mad' as the stories circulating about himself (he may have thought) included his strange adventures surely would have been known in England too, and they were, as will be shown.

Perhaps Walpole did not read newspapers but only listened to the 'Town Cryer', but the local interesting magazines certainly ran articles on this odd individual. However, for the most part, almost all the comments from various sources regarding St Germain showed that he had overawed many people and has left an indelible impression o them.

A certain Prince Karl Von Hessekassel said of St Germain that, "He was the greatest philosopher that ever lived". Quite an accolade, one wonders how many philosophers he knew? Nevertheless, the different impressions he made on various people are quite notable.

He was referred to as an adventurer and a 'jacobite' of England, living as he did, during the days of The French Pretender, Bonnie Prince Charlie, when attempting to take the English throne. He may have been thought of as English due to his wide knowledge and fluency in other languages. Perhaps this is why that, at one point, the French Police thought he was a Russian spy, possibly because he was overheard speaking Russian.

Another comment made about St Germain again, in the positive mode, stated that "He was a good soul, upright, valiant and worthy of admiration and that he knows everything" (agreeing, in this last phrase with Voltaire). This opinion was expressed by Johann Karl Phillip Cobend (1712 – 1770).

Certainly, one of the highest accolades (if not the highest) any person could receive would be, to be classified as someone who 'knew everything' (if that was indeed possible). The only person who could state such a thing with regard to another person, would have to know everything themselves.

Of course, there would be a more 'down to earth' explanation we could offer, and that is, that St Germain could discuss and portray knowledge of any subject or topic that came up for discussion.

However, one thing is quite clear and that is, that Count St Germain made a distinct impression on anyone he ever met in many other countries.

There was a Danish Diplomat who was living in France at the time of St Germain. He was known as Baron Charles Henri de Gleichman (to name but a few) and he clearly stated, that St Germain once showed him a substantial quantity of precious stones, the majority of which were diamonds, quite an abundance of jewels but also some coloured diamonds.

All of the diamonds and jewels seemed to be perfect examples of their type. It was not stated at this time by St Germain that he had made them but from what we are learning this maybe so, as no one could ever state that he ever visited a jeweller in order to purchase any of them.

The only jeweller that St Germain was ever recorded as visiting was the jeweller to King Louis XV himself, which will be related in due course. It soon became clear that it was not just hearsay or gossip regarding St Germain's ability to somehow manufacture and refine the perfect examples of precious stones, or his alleged ability to transmute base metals into gold and silver.

St Germain's ability in this regard was said to have been actually witnessed by a certain Marquis De Valbelle. He had paid a visit (or perhaps was invited) to the laboratory of St Germain, which was no doubt quite substantive and well equipped and certainly would be part of the Great Chateau that King Louis had provided for him.

St Germain at this point (perhaps somewhat uncomfortable) realised that more and more people as was apparent in Valbelle's visit, both male and female (his elixir of youth) were hearing of his prowess in these skills and continued to appear on the scene looking for proof or confirmation of his alleged wondrous powers.

However, as will be shown, when things 'got too hot' for Germain he would simply disappear from the scene and show up in some other country, but in this case, De Valbelle was shown, without any obvious signs of trickery a close up demonstration of ST Germain's skills.

The Count, during this demonstration, asks De Valbelle for a silver coin, Valbelle then offered a six-franc silver piece to St Germain. Valbelle watched St Germain closely after he took the coin.

St Germain was seen to apply or cover the silver coin with some kind of black substance, the Count then was observed to immerse the coin into the heat of the furnace.

Valbelle was intently watching for any signs of trickery or subterfuge, never took his eyes off the process, finally, when St Germain removed the coin from the furnace, cooled, cleaned off any residue of soot or the black substances he had covered it with, he showed it to Valbelle, who was wide eyed in wonderment. The coin was clearly no longer silver but was of pure gold. Certainly, Valbelle needed no more convincing and went away, no doubt bursting to tell his story of what he had witnessed, to the first friend he met.

Nevertheless, this was not the only instance where St Germain would demonstrate his skills to certain people he chose to allow to witness them openly. St Germain performed a similar operation of transmutation to a certain Casanova De Seinhalt.

For all his obvious abilities to transmute different metals into gold, which is astounding enough to those who have not studied the alchemists art. To manufacture diamonds, is clearly, quite a different matter. Yet St Germain seemed so casual about it. But surely he must have known that he had laid himself open to every criminally minded person or cutthroat gangs of murderers who would go out of their way to capture him and force him to reveal his methods on pain of death, but being so friendly with the King, one would have thought that King Louis would have assigned a group of his personal palace guards to accompany St Germain everywhere for maximum protection, after all St Germain represented a valuable investment to the King personally. Furthermore, the King's mistress Madame Pompadour was also quite anxious to ensure St Germain' safety as she still sought his elixir of youth.

To return to the Count's incredible ability to produce diamonds. How could St Germain have known in his time (assuming that he was restricted to a particular time, which does not seem to have been the case), that in order to produce diamonds from carbon, a pressure of 273,200 kilograms per square centimeter is required?

In addition to the enormous pressure that would be required, a temperature of just below 3,000c is needed. In spite of St Germain's cosy connections with the King and their combined wealth, it does not seem very likely that the scientific know-how would have been available generally at the time of St Germain, but he was so unique in so many ways, we cannot be too pedantic about it. His knowledge of all topics seemed to have no bounds.

Nevertheless, as said, with their combined financial resources, the ability to acquire all the specialist equipment, if it was available, would not have been a problem financially in order to commence such an operation.

Whichever way we look at it the whole conception is nothing short of miraculous, but it does not end there. St Germain was also alleged to have had the ability to rectify flaws in diamonds and cause them to disappear. He himself only possessed flawless diamonds.

During St Germain's close association with Louis XV, a lengthy discourse was held, along with some Lords, who obviously would be close associates of the King and St Germain and almost certainly sworn to secrecy regarding St Germain and his abilities, in particular his skills in removing flaws from diamonds.

During this restricted debate, the King sent for a reasonably large diamond that contained a flaw. One gets the impression on face value, particularly with other witnesses present, to have been purposely contrived by Louis to ensure that St Germain would have to 'put his money where his mouth is' regarding the removal of flaws in diamonds. At that point, and somewhat craftily, King Louis casually mentioned to St Germain, that his jeweller had estimated that the current value of his large diamond taking into account the flaw as 6000 livres.

St Germain examined the diamond, then the King added, "Of course, without the flaw, it would no doubt, realise more than 10,000 Livres". At this point, the King probably felt that he had cornered his prey. All eyes were on St Germain.

Clearly, it was a case of "Over to you Monsieur St Germain". Most probably the King fully expected the Count to respond in the sense, that the flaw was too deep or too ingrained and probably too difficult to remove no doubt many eyes witnessed, when St Germain coolly stated, "If you would trust me with this your Highness, I shall return it in about a month's time".

Sure enough, the Count was as good as his word and eventually returned the diamond to an astonished King, with no sign of the flaw present. The King naturally was now interested in the current value of his diamond which now appeared quite flawless. If, that is, if it was the diamond that the King had given to St Germain. The King summoned the jeweller to the Court; the jeweller confidently confirmed the diamond as the King's property and asserted that the flaw had indeed been removed and estimated its current value as now worth around 9,600 livres.

Astoundingly, the Lady in Waiting to Madame Pompadour stated that, "The Count could also culture pearls and make them grow". His abilities regarding pearls, seems to have been widely known, as it was said that he could produce pearls with a fine lustre".

There is a factor of course, that we must consider and it must have been discussed among his contemporaries, that the Count knew someone among his Chinese connections, which could produce the pearls for him, as the art of pearls and their production, was being adopted in China in the 1300s. Indeed, Germain had travelled to the Far East and understood the Chinese Language.

However, I would rather suggest, that given his other obvious talents and abilities, he learned the art there, rather than 'cheating' by pretending, he had produced them.

One of the strange oddities regarding his great wealth was that no one could pin down the source of it, or trace any functioning bank accounts or evidence or traceable income. Since he was such good friends with Louis XV, the King would surely have known the right connections to commission, in order to investigate his wealth, but had it become known to St Germian, his willingness to tutor the King in the arts needed to increase his wealth would be at risk.

It is stated that with regard to the mysterious wealth and lack of traceable income, the London Gazette of 1760 related a story regarding one of the Ministers of France, who apparently became quite suspicious of St Germain and decided to, if it was possible, to expose or somehow discredit him. He discreetly ordered an official enquiry into all (or any) of the supposed remittances and equity from various sources from wherever they may come from.

In this regard, it must have seemed more like a personal vendetta, born out of envy, to the other Ministers, as surely it would have been outside his remit. One would have thought that the decision to mount such an enquiry would have been made under the auspices of the Minister responsible for Customs and Excise or the Office of the Exchequer rather than just a routine Minister 'poking his nose in', as it were.

For example, the Minister for Education enquiring into a private citizens financial affairs.

Nevertheless, an investigation was carried out where St Germain's affairs were scrutinised over a period of some two years, during which, St Germain himself was kept under surveillance and carefully spied upon.

One might have thought that if it was widely known that St Germain could produce silver, pearls and in particular flawless diamonds, then he would have no need of any further wealth or income to be brought into France from another Country. He was quite able to produce his own wealth.

One cannot pay such commodities into a bank account. St Germain must have had many sources where he could sell his created items for cash as he only dealt in cash and paid for everything he needed in cash. The enquiry confirms this but not, one imagines, finding out about his disposal procedures or the countries involved.

St Germain travelled widely and must have had many overseas connections, goldsmiths, jewellers etc. However, the enquiry never discovered any remittances that came into the Kingdom for him, or obviously, his overseas connections, when concentrating solely on what other sources of wealth came in, rather than what St Germain arranged to go out.

All this may help to explain the remark made of him by Frederick the Great, "He is a man that no one was ever been able to understand". We also mentioned Casanova De Seingalt, who recorded in his memoirs that King Louis had confided in him, with regard to St Germain (obviously he was mainly the object of discussion among the group, which should not surprise us) that ST Germain was in the habit of melting down small diamonds in order to create a larger one, and in one case, he melted down a group of small diamonds weighing in at 24 carats in order to produce a larger one that weighed in at 12 carats.

We must consider two important points here, firstly the aforesaid immense scientific processes required to melt down the small diamonds and secondly, more enquiringly, if he always manufactured his own diamonds why did he waste his time producing all those small diamonds only to have to melt them down to obtain a large one, why not produce the large one in the first place? This suggests that he may have obtained the other diamonds from other sources for rings etc.

Which means, of course, it could be said, that if he also manufactured jewellery, such as necklaces and gold rings (although this is never mentioned) he would need smaller diamonds, but it is of little use, our attempts in trying to figure out the Count and his motives when no one in Europe, or indeed many other countries could not.

There seems to have been a fairly tight knit group, who today we may disparagingly call 'The idle rich', that included St Germain, although he was far from idle, who all liked to imbibe together and included in the group were Casanova, the King himself and a few others. The chatter among this group resulted in Casanova mentioning in his memoirs the 'diamond melting' episode. Some others mentioned where the Duc De Deux and a Swede The Compte De Levenhoop who all enjoyed 'supping at Metz'.

Clearly, as well as 'supping', they all enjoyed a good gossip and would probably take advantage of St Germain's absence perhaps on a visit to the loo, to discuss him and his achievements and all of this often resulted in items from various memoirs being able to piece together the activities of St Germain.

The possibility exists that a good deal of the achievements of the Count, especially with regard to his ability regarding diamond creation and manipulation, may have been greatly embellished through no more than drink fuelled chatter but this is too easy an assumption when looking closely at the facts.

Nevertheless, the wealth of King Louis is certainly true, particularly when being combined with that of St Germain and obviously, if the equipment required for the operations in St Germain's laboratory in his Chateau (courtesy of the King) was available then it would not have been a problem to acquire it.

It may be of some relevance to mention here that ornaments made of platinum were found in Ecuador dating back to ancient time, which obviously implies that the natives had the ability to create temperatures of over 1770^c in order to be able to melt it. The United States Bureau of Standards when testing an alloy of an ancient artifact, ascertained that the original dwellers of America must have had furnaces that were capable of developing temperatures of 9,000° seven thousand years ago.

As well as this, an ancient Chinese General, had a metal girdle that was composed in the main, with mostly aluminium. He lived between the years AD 265 and AD 316.

The production of aluminium in the West only began in 1825 by chemical methods. In 1968 Dr Koriut Megurchian of the USSR unearthed over two hundred furnaces that had been in use over four thousand five hundred years ago.

The people worked with all the metals we fabricate and utilise today, they were even knowledgeable about the process of alloying metals together to produce strength without brittleness just as we do today by alternating the amounts of carbon added to steel.

Among the many discoveries, involving metals several pairs of high quality steel tweezers, in other words, 'spring steel' where found. Regarding these documented facts, it would surely be true, that St Germain 'knew everything', that he must have been aware of the advanced capabilities of the ancients and even perhaps studied them intently during his long life and extensive travels throughout other lands.

Almost certainly, rather acting as a 'tourist', he would have headed to the nearest bibliothequt to study the origins, legends, history and the records (if any) regarding the people.

We may recall the King's wish to become a 'pupil' under St Germain's tutelage, but this would have required intensive and prolonged study, which the King could not achieve due to his royal duties in Court and so forth. The King was only assigned a normal lifespan, whereas St Germain had a distinctly lengthy one when amassing all his knowledge.

Nevertheless, the King closely involved himself in the operations and actions of St Germain, but Germain, knowing the value of the secrets that he could impart, he almost certainly withheld certain information but allowed less important data (which may have seemed important to the King) in a 'drip-feed' manner to the King, keeping him interested and satisfied.

St Germain was certainly not going to be too 'free and easy' with regard to information and method that could be used against him.

Nevertheless, St Germain was aware that the gossip about his achievements was spreading so fast throughout the land that no doubt, he was beginning to feel rather uncomfortable about it, but as said, he was aware of the protective cover we had with his relationship with King Louis.

St Germain was well aware that not all the French Ministers were in awe of him or his talents and no doubt would discredit him at the first opportunity. St Germain however, had other powerful friends and associates. He spent five years in The Court of the Shah of Persia, learning the jeweller's craft. He could speak Arabic as well as his fluency in other languages. It was said that he could even speak ancient Greek and Sanskrit.

With regard to his apparent longevity, an elderly 'Countess Von Georgy' had met St Germain fifty years ago and was astonished to find that he still looked the same as he did then. She confronted him regarding this and St Germain said to her "Yes Madam, I am very old". She replied, "Yes but surely not one hundred years old?" St Germain smiled and said, "That is not impossible". St Germain never confirmed very much outright, he seemed to delight in letting them keep guessing (and gossiping), but it must have occurred to him, as suggested, that he was playing a very dangerous game.

His useful association with King Louis and the nobility, was perhaps more fragile than he possibly realised. However, with his social gatherings, imbibing and 'supping', he made sure he stayed within the apparent protection of powerful friends.

It is said that St Germain held a banquet at his chateau (courtesy of King Louis) where his guests where a selection of Lords and various aristocrats. Toward the end of the courses, (perhaps rather ostentatiously) he ensured that along with the dessert, that it was served with a large precious stone on a plate.

Such actions as these most certainly got the tongues wagging. No doubt his guests assume from what they had heard, that t Germain had manufactured the jewels that they received in his laboratory.

There are frequent references made in alchemical literature to the 'philosophers stone', but it is unlikely to have been what we know as a 'stone' but rather, the secrets that would include the recipe for the long sought after 'elixir of youth' and no doubt the secrets of producing diamonds, gold, pearls and so forth.

As 'stone' is made up of various minerals compounded together by the forces within the Earth, washed over and formed by millennia of gravitational attraction heat and weight, then disturbed and forced up through volcanic action and so forth and certain stones may contain many of the minerals along with others, perhaps herbal ingredients that maybe contained in the elusive 'elixir of youth'. It is not so surprising that so many courtly ladies sought the company of St Germain, since the gossip was so rampant, regarding his allegedly continual youthful appearance and his well know abilities in other fields (shared by King Louis).

Clearly the natural assumption was that St Germain had discovered (or manufactured) the elixir they all sought so avidly and indeed may actually be using it himself for what else could explain his 'eternal youth'?

Modern day science will admit that one day a substance or a mixture of substances will be found (or perhaps we could say re-discovered) where a compound of the various vitamins, minerals and other additives could produce amazing results. We only have to consider the substantial amount of laboratories researching away in the private chemical services, functioning for medical research, producing all those liquid potions, tablets and pills and the observation of the results of them, when ingested and made ready and safe for general distribution through tests.

Even though a close watch on such medical and chemical laboratories under the auspices of the Medical Council and Government Guidelines is in force, such laboratories are private enterprises and business and profit orientated organisations.

Because of these factors, it could become possible that enormous financial gain could be realised by 'accidentally' hitting on an amazing discovery that seemed to restore youth and vitality displayed very obviously in a volunteer paid handsomely for taking part as (crudely put) a 'test dummy'.

We must realise that as well as the large amount of private chemical laboratories working for the Health Service, there are also a substantial amount of private pharmaceutical laboratories belonging to and working for the perfume and cosmetic industry, which as everyone is aware, is a major and competitive enterprise.

They may also discover, perhaps accidentally, a product that resulted in amazing and obvious restoration of youth and the re-vitalisation of the skin. Even today, they claim wondrous results in making our wrinkles disappear, but in actuality, such results are very minor.

However, we could imagine a volunteer that was perhaps over forty suddenly being transformed into a twenty year old in appearance as being (financially) 'silenced' and blanket of secrecy descending like the equivalent of a military 'ultra secret' classification.

The financial benefits would be enormous and obvious and the major fear with regard to the company that made the discovery being fearful of industrial espionage, which does occur today. The company would be suddenly transformed into a 'military' type hierarchy with only a select few having the 'the need to know' category. There would be a great fear of 'whistle blowers' or individuals looking for a substantial short term gain (which could be immense) when thinking of the profits to be made. A rival company would set someone up for life to obtain such secrets.

The hypothetical discovery made maybe a face cream in its original form but may well be developed into, first tablet form, then into an ingestible liquid. Enter, 'the elixir of youth'.

With regard to the Count St Germain, during his 'era', or in his case, one might say, 'eras', we may also like to consider that the Count dabbled in cosmetics. The comparisons to the aforesaid are now obvious. Because of this, there were many ladies of the Court who sought to make contact with him and to seek his advice and of course a sample of his products, for which they would pay handsomely. All this of course would clear up the questions of his lack of incoming finances from elsewhere, he probably insisted on cash payments for any services rendered. In this regard, it is rather surprising that the Customs and Excise and Revenue Departments mentioned when the French Minister was snooping into his finances where not pursuing him for non-payment of taxes (assuming a force of Income Tax was in force in his time).

During the life and times of St Germain, it was common place for the Nobles, Dignitaries and so-forth (including the ladies) to write in, one could say "Their diaries", but a more upmarket term would be their "Memoirs" all the interesting events that affected them, or their lives that seemed worth recording, although to us, in modern parlance, it would seem more like an 'ego trip' as they assumed that people would be so interested in them and their lives that they would wish to read them.

Nevertheless, it is for certain that anyone who knew the Count and interacted with him during their lifetime would most assuredly have something to write about than routine gossip.

In one of these memoirs concerning those of a certain Jean Phillips Rameraux, who was a composer of ballet and opera music, that was in Vogue during the life of the Count, made a particular reference to the Count stating that he did actually possess this 'magic elixir' and did in fact give it to his chosen associates on rare occasions. Also in these memoirs, the subject of the Count's alleged 'eternal youth' and longevity came up again. Apparently, St Germain was seen and recognised fifty years ago where he was described as looking about fifty years of age. Rameraux noted that St Germain still looked the same. All this of course, fuelled the fires of suspicion that St Germain did possess the elixir.

When we look at the inter-relations between King Louis, St Germain and Madame Pompadour, it would seem that St Germain never admitted to the King that he did possess the elixir, either that, or the King was very good at keeping secrets, as he certainly did not tell Madame Pompadour of this, not wise to tell a mistress everything.

It is clear, in any event, she did not know, or else she would not have been in pursuit of St Germain in order to ask him outright about his youthful appearance and of the possibility that he had the 'elixir of youth'. She confronted him with all the stories and accounts of those who had met him long ago yet today he had not aged.

St Germain avoided the question about the elixir but as to the question regarding his age and appearance, he admitted to being "eighty five, perhaps". This appears as though the Count was underestimating his true age (if that was ever ascertained) or he was intent on confusing the 'gossips', because rough calculations show that the Count would be nearer to a hundred years old.

It would seem at this point, that Madame de Pompadour was getting a little ruffled about the wise Count's evasiveness, as he knew how to play one off against the other, so to speak.

However, he had, as said, to tread softly by not offending the wrong people. Madame Pompadour was irritated, being so desperate to obtain the elixir that they all sought and began to take the view that St Germain was a charlatan. It would be interesting to know what kind of conversation ensued later between the King and Madame Pompadour. King Louis had also to 'tread softly', as said, regarding St Germain and what he knew about his talents and to be very careful not to disrupt the subject of their vested interests. The King needed St Germain as much as Germain needed the King.

Therefore, the 'impasse' prevailed. No doubt, as St Germain worked feverishly in his well equipped laboratory, the King was in receipt of his share of gold, silver, pearls and jewels into his coffers and certainly would have discouraged any suggestions of quackery with regard to St Germain and to damp down any gossip that St Germain was a charlatan or a fraud, the King would certainly know better. Perhaps to pacify Madame Pompadour he may well have only dwelled upon St Germain's ability to produce such fine cosmetics to divert her interest.

As it turned out, it was mentioned, emanating perhaps from all the prolific 'memoirs', that St Germain did pacify Madame Pompadour 'by preparing exquisite and effective cosmetics for her'. Perhaps St Germain added a little of his other secret ingredients into the face creams, for example, that produced Noticeable results for her.

It may have been, that, although St Germain may not have given her, in present terms, 'the full monty', those that he did provide, were very effective and did noticeably enhance her beauty and she was said to be quite delighted with the results.

St Germain most certainly, had her back on his side. Nevertheless, the buzz around the courtly circles and the nobility continued just as strongly, mostly with the mystery of his true age and this mysterious 'elixir'. Certainly, as we have said, it would be a continuing point of concern to him to have all this unwanted gossip and conjecture disturbing his peace.

One would have thought that this would have been viewed as a good time to depart on one of his frequent trips abroad to 'lie low' for a while and to 'get off the front page', as it where. However, perhaps that was not so easy when considering his close connections with his 'minder' (and pupil) namely King Louis XV.

We mentioned that the Count had close ties with The Shah of Persia, learning the jeweller's craft. This raised an interesting question 'did the Shah also know of the process of manufacturing jewels and diamonds also free of flaws?', If so, Germain would not be the only one rumoured and spoken about regarding this ability, but this did not happen and St Germain remains the only focal point of these stories.

Therefore, St Germain, rather than being a 'pupil' in the 'learning mode' regarding the jewellers craft, would surely have been more of a 'teacher' of these arts. St Germain was also a good friend of Prince Ferdinand Von Lobkowitz and even that of the British General Robert Clive (of India), all of which indicates just how well travelled he was during his lifetime, the length of which, we have not yet fully established.

On top of his other amazing qualities, St Germain was also reputed to be a great healer and was attributed to possess the 'remedies for the infirmities in which time triumphs over the human fabric'. In other words, other 'by products' of his elixir of youth.

By this time, the Count is beginning to sound more and more like another very notable character from history that is 'Apollonius of Tyana'. I covered the story of his outstanding character in my book 'Pillars of Fire' (Arena Publications) which we will cover in due course.

Among his other adventures, the Count was said to have taken part in the 'coup d'état' that resulted in Catherine the Great taking the Throne of Russia.

In spite of all these 'overseas' adventures where his 'acceptance' appeared to be so natural as though he had some strange right to be involved, he still found the time to pursue his talents and his experiments in the alchemical arts.

One wonders how much gold now lies in the coffers of France, the Bank of England and even in Fort Knox that may have originated from the furnaces of St Germain. It would have been a great advantage for St Germain to have his laboratory in the Chateau courtesy of King Louis, who no doubt assigned a contingency of guards along with it, than an area more vulnerable, to carry out his work. Obviously, it would have been in the King's interest to provide good protection of his investment.

Nevertheless, the Count still managed to show up in Berlin, Italy, Corsica and Tunis. Most certainly, at that time, no one could be more 'worldly wise' or so well travelled, as the Count and his fluency in so many other languages would have been a great advantage to him. But some of the reports regarding the Count do seem hard to accept and some of the accounts that originated through the various 'memoirs' may have been over embellished by the writers to heighten the drama of their stories, so, one must wonder about the authenticity of some of them.

If the origins of the Count where accurate when referring to Transylvania in around 1690, then the account regarding him stating that in 1776 he wore the uniform of a Russian General, would make him about eighty years old. Nevertheless, it was stated that St Germain was the guest of Count Orloff, when the Russian Navy was anchored at the time off Livorno in Italy.

It was stated that the Orloff brothers always spoke of him with high regard and of the important role; he played in the Russian Revolution. We must ask, "Was there anywhere that the Count did not show up in, or influence in any way?"

The Count was also involved in the Masonic and Rosicrucian rituals when we mentioned Prince Karl von Hesse Kassel, which was described as St Germain's friend, protector and 'disciple', the word disciple infers, just as with King Louis, that he was also a keen follower of the alchemical arts. Anyone who was capable, or alleged to do all the things that were attributed to St Germain would, quite naturally, have many disciples.

Among his many other talents, St Germain was an accomplished violinist and at least Horace Walpole (as we previously said) was gracious enough to bestow that compliment upon him before his rather disparaging remarks that St Germain was 'mad and not very sensible'. From all that we know of St Germain, it is hard to understand why that would be said of him. Along with all his other activities and his foreign travels, it is quite amazing that he found the time to compose musical renderings for the violin.

Music publishers of the time, such as 'Walsh of London', would not be interested in just one rendering, so it follows that Germain must have submitted a substantial amount of musical sheets to them. This event is significant in that it denotes another date, which is 1780, and by this time St Germain would have been around ninety years of age, yet there was no sign of him showing any indications of slowing down in his activities.

There is some interesting information about the Count that was included in a book by Andrew Tomas that was published around fifty years ago which contains some information (although sketchy), about the death of the Count.

Andrew Tomas stated that in Germany at a place called Eckernförde, there is a register that gives us a little information about the Count but does record his death, which is said to have occurred on February 27th in 1784 and clearly mentions his name and also that he was privately interred there but concluded with 'further information unknown'.

However, for all that, the mystery surrounding St Germain continues, simply because the Count shows up yet again in 1785, a year after he was supposed to have been interred at Eckinförde. We could ask "Did he fake his own death?" However, if that was so, one would have thought that he would have 'lowered his profile', so to speak, but the opposite is true in that he allegedly took part in a Masonic conference in 1785, which is said to be a matter of record.

A work titled 'Freumauver Brüderschaft in Frank Reich (France) Vol. 2 page 9, states that, "Among the Freemasons invited to the great conference at Williselmsbad on February 15th 1785, we find St Germain along with St Martin (Count?) and many other notables".

Things become even more incredible as we read on, "The Comtesse De Genlis (Stephanie Felicity) who lived from 1746 to 1830, says that she met Count St Germain in 1821 in Vienna". As we have said, most of the notables wrote of their life experiences in their memoirs, assuming their often-dreary pampered and uninteresting lives would be of interest to many.

However, the snippet came from the memoirs of the above-mentioned Stephanie Felicity; it seems that anything to do with the Count (St Germain) was worth writing about. however, for all these memoirs, what of St Germain himself and his memoirs? Assuming that he ever found time to write any. That would certainly be a very good read.

We cannot say that the above-mentioned Lady Stephanie Felicity fitted the description of a pampered gossip as she was said to have written more than eighty books and also received a pension from Napoleon I.

But in spite of all the memoirs, where they chose to write of things that they thought worthy of recording the fact is that they contributed greatly to the widespread gossip that was rippling not only through France with regard to ST Germain and of course all Europe, it also reached out across the Channel to the Courtly circles of England.

Among the ladies of the various Courts and castles, they where all of a flutter about the possible existence of this wondrous 'elixir of youth' that they had heard about and naturally were all most interested on how they could obtain it.

As St Germain was so coy about it, when he was approached directly, it seemed that he chose those people very carefully whom he wished to bestow with his precious product. Wealth and position did not impress him, he was seemingly more interested in their characters.

Many of the ladies of high standing were all attracted like wasps to a jam pot to St Germain 'who else?' after all the widespread gossip all centered around him and so all the ladies that where fearful of losing their youthful and desirable appearance where all quite desperate to obtain the elixir 'at any price'. Of course, St Germain could have read into this, that 'any price' could possibly also mean that certain ladies where willing to trade their virtue for it, but it does not seem that St Germain (although he could have been quite selective and take his pick) was of such a character that could be described in his day as a 'cad and a bounder'.

Nevertheless many of the ladies made it clear to St Germain that he only needed to 'name his price'. Obviously, this elixir was a source of great power to the holder, not to mention the other attributes accorded to St Germain.

As we had said, stories regarding the mysterious and enigmatic Count were not only circulating throughout Europe, the London Chronicle ran a story dealing with the alleged abilities and all the amazing accounts that were buzzing throughout the land regarding the Count.

Naturally, most of the gossip and stories centered around this mysterious elixir that he had discovered (or more likely concocted). In the aforesaid newspaper story, it was stated, that a certain Duchess (not named) wrote to the Count stating "They tell me that you have that inestimable secret that is worth more than all your gold and wealth to us, that is, the medicine that will restore youth. Please let me have it as soon as possible" (she must have been growing older by the minute). She finished by stating "Name your own conditions".

St Germain was, as we have said, usually quite evasive when approached in this manner, either directly or by letter that smacked of desperation and he replied in response to the letter by the Duchess, "Those who do have these secrets (implying that he did not) do not choose that it should be known that they have them".

The Count was being very crafty in his reply as it could have taken some of the pressure off himself and inferred that he was not the one to pursue.

However, the account in the London Chronicle infers that the Duchess did not give up so easily. It stems that perhaps through further correspondence and agreement, St Germain was accommodating to the Duchess.

What follows in the Chronicle story would seem more believable if the Duchess had been named, because of it's high strangeness! However, the old adage, 'why bother about the facts if is a good story', no doubt prevailed in the newspapers of the time, just as fake news allegations prevails so much today.

Be that as it may, it says that the Count brought a phial of four or five spoonfuls to the Duchess and made it clear that just ten drops would be sufficient and to take care not to waste it as "It would not be easy to get a further supply".

Various assumptions can be read into this, firstly, that the Count (in modern parlance) was only the 'pusher' and not the supplier, and secondly that to obtain more may necessitate extensive travel to a certain foreign land to obtain the various ingredients that he required to concoct it. One could imagine him hacking his way through dense foliage to find the secret herbs and plants and thirdly, that because of the previously mentioned remarks, it may take the pressure off him to some extent, as it would infer that he was not the manufacturer.

Most certainly, carrying this rare and expensive substance around in a glass phial would be rather like handling a glass phial of nitro glycerine, with the same fear of dropping it.

However, the Duchess had finally obtained her elixir (and as the Chronicle story goes on), she places it among her other potions and remedies into her medical cabinet. The Lady in Waiting to the Duchess naturally had free reign in and around the Duchess's apartments. The story goes that the (said) Lady in Waiting was seized with colic one day and not being able to approach the Duchess for her possible assistance, as she was not in residence, she took the liberty of entering into the boudoir of the Duchess, thinking she may find a cure for her discomfort, she noticed this phial and its liquid within that stated it could be ingested, she took hold of it and noted its pleasant fragrance.

She wondered if she dare take it, but as the Duchess was away on an engagement she drank most of it down, feeling that it surely would not be missed and in any case, the Duchess could easily get more. She was pleased to find that the relieving effect as so immediate and happily went about her duties

When the Duchess finally returned, tired and ready to rest of the night, she summoned her Lady in Waiting. She was startled, when a female appeared who clearly was not her woman.

"Child, who are you, how came you here, get out". Her woman curtseyed and replied "Your Grace speaks to me in an uncommon manner you surely must know that I have the honour to be your Grace's woman and I am here to attend to you". The Duchess, astonished said "You my woman?, Child, my woman is five and forty in age, I dare swear, that you have not yet reached sixteen".

Apparently, France was all of a buzz regarding this story that obviously travelled across the Channel and into the lap of the Editor of the Chronicle. One could imagine the Count being quite furious about this, as the Duchess would have been seen so careless with the potion.

He would not be in the vein to re-supply her, but whether it had anything to do with the story, the Count adopted one of his disappearing acts and the Duchess was unable to get a further supply of the wonder drug and became 'grey and elderly and totally unfulfilled'.

Keeping in mind the obvious longevity enjoyed by the Count and the fact that various notables throughout the decades testified to the fact that he always looked the same no matter which decade he appeared in, we cannot discount the previous story too easily, after all, if a man like Voltaire was moved to say "He is a man that knows everything and never dies", he must have been capable of achieving great things.

We have more memoirs to refer to. We should say rely on to put the case' for St Germain and his exploits and indeed his very existence, such written documentation is essential to prevent us from simply writing him off as a myth or just a 'tall story'.

We have said that after his escapade with the Duchess and the adverse publicity with all the gossip rumbling around, which we cannot blame the people to0 much for, as it was certainly a story worth repeating. St Germain may have thought that it was a good time to make himself scarce.

This is borne out by a certain Franz Graffer in his 'memoirs of Vienna'. He quotes a statement from St Germain as follows, "I will set out tomorrow evening and then I shall disappear from Europe and go to the Himalayas". One might assume that this was just 'big talk' by St Germain, simply out to impress, but the character profile that is emerging regarding St Germain this conclusion just does not fit.

I mentioned certain similarities to another enigmatic character known as Apollonius of Tyana he also travelled to the Himalayas to meet 'the men who knew everything', a phrase often used when describing St Germain.

When dealing with these strange similarities to St Germain and Apollonius of Tyana, the latter lived during the era of Jesus and the data on St Germain (updated in 2018) by Stephen Wagner in regard to St Germain's origins stated that he was alive at the time of Jesus, although he qualified it by Saying that that some of these accounts should be taken less seriously (we will happily comply).

Nevertheless, St Germain's studies encompassed the secret Temples of Egypt, to the Tibetan Monasteries and much between. In the Bibliotheque de-Troyes there exists a manuscript that is said to be the only known compilation written by St Germain and is preserved there. This is strange in itself, as with all his known experiences and knowledge, one would have thought that he had the ability to write, regarding a whole range of subjects and ought to have done so, particularly as one of his contemporaries of high standing was said to have written over eighty books, whose life was in no way as full and of such varied experiences as St Germain himself. We refer to the Comtesse De Genlis mentioned also, as Stephanie Felicity, particularly since St Germain seems to have done everything and accomplished everything, we should not be surprised to learn that he travelled in space, well, as a matter of fact he did. At least he did, according to the above-mentioned manuscript. It is said to contain a number of illustrated symbols and diagrams of an enigmatic nature, but more astounding is the text that follows:- "The velocity with which we sped through space, can be compared with nought but itself". This phrase is understandable, when the fastest speed in his time would be a horse on the racecourse.

However, the text continues "In an instant, I had lost sight of the plains below and the Earth became like a vague cloud, I had been lifted to a great height, for quite a long time, I rolled through space and I observed globes revolving all around me and other earths gravitate at my feet".

The above account is taken from 'We are Not the First' by Andrew Tomas. It certainly reads like an account of an experience in space. The more cynical among us may assume, that he wrote it after imbibing, perhaps in some of the more exotic 'magic mushrooms' he may have found during his extensive Eastern travels.

Of course, we could assume that St Germain was influenced before writing this account by ancient writings such as the four thousand seven hundred year old 'Epic of Etana' that contains a poem of the flight of Etana allegedly born aloft by a huge 'eagle'. The eagle told Etana to look down at various points when they ascended higher and higher, so high in fact that after the third hour the Earth was likened to a speck of dust.

There are other references that St Germain may have been aware of, particularly with regard to his travels in Egypt. An extract from the Egyptian *Book of the Dead* states, "This place has no air, its depth is unfathomable and it is black as the blackest night".

Nevertheless, St Germain's account certainly reads like an account of space travel and a lot further than the Moon but around the planets themselves. It is a pity that St Germain did not enlighten us from which 'spaceport' he departed from or, who assisted him in this epic adventure, but we are becoming used to being amazed by his alleged adventures and statements. The next of which is no less astounding:- "I am more needed in Constantinople, than in England, there, to prepare two inventions which you will have in the next Century which will be steam trains and steamboats".

Apparently, this was stated to the aforementioned Franz Graffer, where we referred to his 'memoirs of Vienna'. We have said that it is tempting to write off the whole saga of the Count St Germain but we are prevented from doing so by these actual characters and notables from history that did exist, including (we hope) their memoirs. We certainly cannot write off Voltaire as having 'imagined' the Count and his exploits. All these traceable characters are so deeply interwoven in the work, we have to accept the core validity of the story, but we still have to consider the many possible embellishments that may have been added to the accounts as people wished to impress others. Although the secrets of alchemy and the so-called elixir of life seem mythical, science has to pay more attention to these historic tales as science itself knows that we are getting ever closer to the ability to perhaps 'rearrange' the atomic number of matter and the periodic table shows us just how close the various elements are to each other on the subject of alchemy, gold, silver lead etc. however, the subject of longevity will be dealt with in the chapter on Noah and the immense almost incredible ages of the biblical patriarchs, so 'matter of factly' mentioned in Genesis, allegedly written by Moses who seemed so sure of them. One would not expect that St Germain, in spite of his wondrous accomplishments, to have anyone daring to suggest that St Germain had discovered the 'Double Helix' and the genetic code and the complete knowledge of the human genome, but that is where the secrets of ageing will be found. Discoveries in this field are rapidly increasing as time goes by and certain speculations have been made, such as it is 'frightening what we are discovering'. Why frightening? Does this once again display inborn fear of the unknown? Why not 'it is encouraging' to discover facts that may help humanity, simply because once we have cracked the code, that is, the entire human genome, with the ability to 'control and manipulate' every gene then we will be on the road to eliminate all human maladies even the process of ageing.

If St Germain had discovered the process of eliminating or, more probably, 'slowing' the process, it would most likely have been due to St Germain discovering and manipulating and experimenting with rare herbs and plants. Medical science is now well aware of the benefits of foxglove digitals in heart cases, but how did the ancients know this? It could only be through centuries of trial and error experimentation but how much writing and recording and logging of this information took place? In addition, how much was destroyed, although genetic discoveries have positive implications, there is a 'downside' when we consider the negative aspects of the human psyche, and whether the ability to manipulate the negative genes would have good results. This could be like a dangerous weapon falling into the wrong hand in order to create 'cyborgs'. Considerations of this nature give rise to films and stories such as the X-Files with the creation of 'terminators' but to return to the elixir of youth and longevity. It is not just a simple task of identifying just a single gene, controlling certain human features, such as excessive height or lack of it, several gene pairs have to work in unison. In a fictional work by Jane Goldman, a certain Dr Ridley said, "The man who controls the fountain of youth controls the world", but 'youth' implies inexperience, real power and control is usually manipulated by those who have left youth behind them and control through experience gained during their lives. St Germain would seem to have been on the right track, when seeking immortality. However, the whole subject of gene experimentation and research must bring with it a need for a set of ethical rules and some form of control, but this does not prevent the studies and perhaps experiments from continuing in this fastest growing sciences (as it has been called) today.

As well as pursing the quest for longevity, it is also necessary to attempt to prevent the opposite affliction, that is, premature ageing often displayed in children (Progeria) caused by gene mutation, which is being studied and in the pursuance of a cure, a side effect or discovery to solve the problem of ageing may be found during intensive research. There is an interesting statement that was made to Professor Stephen A Grawetz of the Wayne State University School of Medicine, "We are assuming that the genes related to Progeria or ageing prematurely, indicate that the control force or mechanism has been lost, so that if we target all the genes related to ageing at once, turn them off and let normal development proceed, so you do not age anymore. If you could stop the process of ageing then at that point you may have discovered the secrets of eternal youth. The Count St Germain, if he did live as long as is believed (backed up by confirmation of historical figures who did exist) then, as said, his secret may have lain in the studies of herbal and natural growths. He travelled extensively and could have easily developed a wide range of medical cures to boot when working on his elixir.

We have said that any legend, whether written or in the shape of a person, can be affected by both positive and negative factors over time, but St Germain traversed through time and kept his unique aura and reports of his accomplishments never changed. The story of the Count may be classified as unbelievable, but must be believed, simply because of the substantial amount of well placed individuals who are not fictitious, who he came in contact with, not just in France but all over the world. In addition, because of the above factors, no one can say that the whole affair is nothing but a hoax. This is all very well but there is no one around from Biblical times who can testify that his longevity reached back into the time of Christ and that he even attended the wedding feast at Cana, it is a step too far to expect anyone to believing that, yet it did appear in an article titled 'Saint Germain the Immortal Count', by Stephen Wagner.

St Germain knew the infamous Giacomo Girolamo Casanova, who stated that the Count told him in an almost casual manner, that he was three hundred years old. It is also recorded that on returning to France from one of his many adventures, in 1774 he warned Louis XVI and Marie Antoinette of the forthcoming French Revolution and that it would occur in fifteen years time, the Count seems to have been an accomplished prophet as well as his other talents because that prophesy certainly came to pass. The Comtesse D'adhémar recognised the Count in 1820 and commented that he appeared as a man in his mid-forties . We appear to be moving into the realms of the unbelievable again, when we refer to another case regarding St Germain's obvious longevity, yet supported by a traceable figure in the form of Albert Van Dam, who conversed with the Count and stated that St Germain had known Nero, Dante and other notables of history. We have said that St Germain clearly had great wealth and resources yet, no one could ever trace any information on any bank accounts he held. How was this man so unique in history or made such an impression through the decades (one might almost say centuries)? Why just one man? However, of all the worlds' peoples, no one can compare any other individual to him or highlight their abilities as coming even close to his incredible person. He was involved with politics and not just in his own country, he was present in procedures involving other countries affairs including major political decisions, for example, advising the Commander of the Imperial Russian Army in their conflict with Turkey, which the Russians did win.

He had already (as we have mentioned) been complicit in placing Catherine the Great on the throne in 1762. St Germain was also, as said, they have been linked to various known secret societies such as the Asiatic Brothers, The Knights of Light, The Illuminati and even The Grand Order of Templar's. The term 'mesmerised' i.e. hypnotised, stems from the name Anton Mesmer.

St Germain was seen in Germany with Mesmer and it was claimed that Anton Mesmer's talents where entirely due to St Germain's coaching and providing him with the necessary techniques to pursue his career.

Finally, a recorded article concerning the famed member of the Theo physical Society, Helen Blavatsky, from 1880 to 1900 claimed St Germain was alive and well and was working toward the 'spiritual Development of the West'. There is alleged to be a genuine photograph taken of Blavatsky and St Germain together. What more can we say after the welter of information that has been brought to bear on this amazing individual. Will there ever be another like him?

CHAPTER II

AM I REALLY DEAD ?

The so called 'near death experience' N.D.E., is now established from alleged dreams, into the realms of reality. It has been accepted by the medical profession as an 'occurrence' defying sometimes, a medical explanation.

Here, we move into considerations of a spiritual nature with regard to some of the strange events that the person affected experiences.

Frequently, the person affected has been on the operating table, where the medical team are mostly convinced, that after frantic attempts at resuscitation that they have lost their patient. Then the patient displays all the necessary symptoms of death yet later completely recovers and begins to relate an amazing story of their experience that seemed to take place completely outside of their body, that 'had medically' died.

These occurrences have happened when in medical terms, the lengthy time involved from the resuscitation attempts to the return to consciousness should have resulted in brain damage, due to the brain being deprived of oxygen for such a lengthy period yet the patient fully regains all their faculties with no sign of any adverse effects due to their 'absence'.

Sometimes surgeons after disposing of all their 'rational' explanations, have to 'think outside the box' as it were and have actually written books on the subject that was obviously impressed them.

They highlight factors such as the patient relating things they have seen or could not have known about as well as dealing initially with the medical side of the phenomena where the patient defies all the medical criteria regarding death, they are forced to move into the realms of the spiritual.

The eternal questions of life after death has been frequently (sometimes heatedly) debated with conclusions made, not in unison, but only in the mind of the person taking part in the debate to suit their own opinion and conclusions.

The cold scientific viewpoint held by many, is that death is final, the end, and that a wish for it to be otherwise is just that 'a wish'. Obviously, to devout religious people, there is no need for any kind of debate to ponder over. Death is the road we all have to take, sooner or later. We pass on, meet our maker, or judged accordingly and then become assigned to our temporary or final residence. The temporary residence is described variously as purgatory or limbo, the final 'heaven' or 'hell'.

STRANGE REALITIES

The permanent residences of course are heaven, if you are lucky enough to go straight there or hell, if you are equally unlucky. Purgatory, as the word suggests, is the place you go to when you are required to be purged or cleansed of your past misdemeanors in order to be eventually paroled before going onto a better place.

In limbo or purgatory, part of the process would ensure that you are forced to reflect on all the beastly things you have done in life and get your nose thoroughly rubbed in them, but at least one can look forward to an eventual 'graduation' after all the naughtiness has been purged from your 'soul'. For the other place, however, it is a 'one way' ticket with no hope of parole or release.

The ancient and established conception of hell is largely unacceptable today, when we conjure up a picture of a horned devil, with cloven hoofs, gleefully pitch forking people into the flames who had grossly sinned, but we should not feel too relieved or feel unconcerned about our naughtiness and just continue our lives in the same old way. There are many versions of hell. For example, if one had been gregarious, outgoing and full of life and enjoyed mixing with, and meeting people in social gatherings, pubs, clubs and so-forth, and suddenly had to spend an eternity among dull morose people with nothing to say, however, even if you had been a fine fellow in some respects, you may still be a murderer and that would be your punishment.

But with regard to heaven, it is said (but not how they found out) that there are various grades of heaven and that there are different stages that one has to pass through, until one reaches the final level, (seventh heaven?) where you are finally seen to meet your maker. Would it be a warm loving light with a divine creator shining out from the centre? Or perhaps (in popular culture) a group of grey aliens with large eyes telling you "Yes, you are right, we are your makers, we did it fifty thousand of your years ago, here is your ticket, go out to that big silvery disc out there and we will take you into the light".

Even if you had been a notorious hit man in real life but still liked to hug your grandson, meet your dubious friends and acquaintances for a pint and to discuss your next victim, go outside for a smoke, you may have smoked heavily in life and still had the craving but had to watch others puffing away and even made to smell the tobacco every day for eternity.

If a person had been thoroughly evil in life, they may have to face an eternity reviewing their past evil deeds. It is hard to imagine the Hitler's, Himmler's, Stalin's or even serial child killers ever finding themselves moving on to a higher level and a chance to become a member of the ultimate club just for saying sorry for a while.

However, to return to the whole concept of the N.D.E. perhaps the release of the spiritual body from the carnal body when you are pronounced medically dead yet float off to begin your N.D.E. is the point when the soul leave the body but may still be able to return.

The human body in life is said to be an 'energy field' but whereas the body can be killed, the energy field cannot and simply transforms into the spirit or soul or another form of energy, but the spirit can still remain in the earthly sphere. This may be simply to have us endure a period of reflection and accept that you are really dead.

Even if we see ourselves as righteous and upstanding and an all round 'good egg', this does not mean that we immediately start to rub shoulders with saints, popes or Mother Teresa. We may have to (as said); earn our promotion by serving a period of genuine repentance. Nobody is perfect; we must all at least have a handful of sins to repent for.

It is believed that the soul or spirit can be jerked out of the body so quickly, perhaps in a fatal car crash, for example, that the person (victim) believes they are still alive and when finally realising that they are dead, they may wander between Earth and a different realm, unless someone can assist them to pass on or 'go into the light'. They may be able to bring this about by haunting a particular place or dwelling until those on the receiving end, bring in a paranormal group to do the honours, some of whom possess quite sophisticated pieces of electronic detection equipment.

When it comes to troublesome spirits, who may, as we have said, want some kind of release from their limbo in Earth space, they would like very much to 'go to the light'. Some members of the medical teams and surgeons in the operating theatres have accepted (possibly being 'at odds' with their colleagues over it) that they can no longer accept the 'closed mind' view, that death (medical death) is final.

To believe this, requires the acceptance that the physical energy of the body transforms into a spirit or soul. One case that I can recall came from a nursing home. One very elderly lady near death raised herself up on one elbow and with the other arm raised up as tough reaching for someone's hand lay down peacefully and passed away with a smile on her face. Naturally, there is always an opposing view. For example there seems to be an interim period, although the signs of medical death had all been shown, the person had not actually died and that the brain, sensing the terminating of the life functions produces a comforting 'last gasp' to comfort the body before final termination and produces the scenario that the person may have heard about beforehand in order to ease the process of final extinction.

STRANGE REALITIES

One of the books written that dealt with the N.D.E. phenomena relates to the case of a lady who was rushed to hospital and required immediate surgery. She showed all the usual pattern of symptoms indicating death. The medical team frantically tried their best to revive and resuscitate her but to no avail. This was a classic case of an apparently deceased person returning to tell the story of their experiences while seemingly out of the body, having transformed into another form of energy which could be deemed the 'soul' or spirit.

The lady had, by all medical terms, been classified as dead. Medical teams in the operating theatres are quite used to this and physically carry out all the attempts at resuscitating, up to a certain time when the decision according to medical signs must be made. Certain cases, such as this event, sometimes defy the established set of rules and return to consciousness apparently no worse for their experience.

In the case of this lady, she excitedly related her story. She had sensed that she was leaving her body and felt herself floating above the operating table and looking down at the medical team attempting to revive her. This must be interpreted as the critical point when the bodily energy field transforms into spiritual energy and the 'soul' departs from the body. It may be experienced by everyone but of course (almost) everyone never returns to describe it.

In the lady's case, she slowly drifted through the walls of the building and observed different people and places (she had not been to this hospital before). This event seems to be a very strong case for the existence of the soul or the spirit that lives on after bodily death simply because the details she related could be and where checked out.

The lady could clearly recall many details, such as observing a woman in the waiting room weeping, holding a bunch of flowers, her clothing that she wrote etc., things she could not have possibly known. Eventually, after a certain period of time the spirit seems to rush back into the body astounding the medical team, who were about the pull the sheet over her face and summon the orderlies to take her to the morgue.

After such a lengthy period of time since her life functions were seen to have been terminated the surgical crew felt sure that at the very least due to lack of oxygen during her spiritual experiences that she would be permanently brain damaged.

However, this lady eventually recovered as though she had merely been asleep. All her senses and faculties were completely restored and she excitedly relayed her experiences that must surely cause a few cocked eyebrow and serious glances among the medical crew.

It is curious and convincing events, such as this case that prompt some doctors and surgeons to write accounts of them for publication and they present a strong case for the validity of the phenomena.

There is an interesting comparison to the above N.D.E. to the claims by some 'abductees' in the UFO phenomena where alleged ETs take the subdued victim to their craft by moving through solid walls. This suggests that such beings could induce in the victim and themselves a form of alternative energy where the atoms of the body are somehow spread out, as are the atoms of the apparently solid wall and quite easily pass through each other. An analogy could be offered where two apparently dense clusters of stars in a colliding galaxy pass through another galaxy where the astronomers ought to be observing exploding stars due to collisions, but this does not seem to be the case. However, with regard to the N.D.E. phenomena, other cases similar with regard to the salient points have occurred and no amount of seemingly logical medical explanations hold good. Also, as said, senior medical people have put their own reputations and their credibility and of course their careers on the line.

In some cases, the patients, when relating their particular experiences, go further than the case just related and appear to reach a point, almost of no return. A 'tunnel' is frequently mentioned, where the person passes through, often seeing a light ahead that they are quickly approaching, and a bright inviting light is experienced. Suddenly, the person is surrounded by people they feel them know who seem to be welcoming them with open arms and a warm loving feeling is experienced. Then suddenly, the visitor is made aware that they must go back and very quickly they are back in the body, back onto the operating table.

The patient often states that to find themselves back into their body is a disappointment rather than a joyful relief that they are still alive. Their experience had been so profound they even became tearful but one interesting point emerged and that was they no longer had any fear of death but actually looked forward to it (which seems to be a little disturbing) but it would depend on the person's circumstances. To someone living alone with few friends and relatives this may seem logical enough. However, to others, perhaps returning to a loving wife or husband and children would surely not harbour these thoughts.

People who have a morose fear of death, thinking it is the end of things and one cannot expect a pleasant change to look forward to, should perhaps remember the words of Jesus himself, who stated , "To conquer death, you only have to die". To many, this would seem strangely contradictory but obviously it just means that a spiritual existence is awaiting everybody, but some would ask, why then did God create us in the first place, just to plod through our "Three score and ten to attain what we could have had in the first place?"

However, we will leave that to the philosophers. One of the most perplexing issues, from the medical point of view, is the accepted 'life' of the brain when death is near, either in a terminal medical case, or simply due to extreme old age.

When death signs appear, the time factor, with regard to oxygen starvation is deemed as critical when the person exhibits the beginning of the process from loss of consciousness and stops breathing. The natural reaction of the medical team and indeed their duty is to attempt to prolong and preserve life rather than to just observe the process. Of course, the medical team could be relieved of this process if the patient had taken steps to state 'Do not resuscitate' for example. When breathing stops, after unconsciousness and the body exceeds the accepted parameters, then brain death and eventually bodily death are (mostly) inevitable.

I say 'mostly' because the N.D.E. experiences appear to defy the logical processes. However, when the usual procedures are completed this enables the death certificate to be compiled.

The problem is, that not only are these critical factors overcome with ease in a person returning from an N.D.E. all the life signs not only return to normal but are in some cases 'enhanced' and the person suddenly has abilities that they did not previously possess. In my book *The Human Enigma* (Arena Publications) I related the story regarding the case of Mellon Thomas Benedict, and since it is relevant to the subject dealt with in this chapter I will mention it again.

As we have said, there are various surgeons and doctors who do accept the 'out of the body experience' phenomena including the possibility of the spirit or 'soul' actually leaving the mortal body. After a thorough analysis of the information that the subject related on being fortunate to have returned to their body (some have even viewed it as unfortunate). We have mentioned the 'alien connection', regarding the new form of the body (the spirit) in abduction cases, and it seems there is a correlation between some ET close encounter reports of the third kind, where the interaction between alleged aliens and the victims, who often refer to the ET as 'being of light'. Those who experience the out of the body phenomena, describe certain features that others have also mentioned, that is the familiar 'tunnel' they appear to be passing through and in the distance is this warm comforting and welcoming feeling with 'being of light' surrounding them.

This experience could well have given rise to the expression 'the light at the end of the tunnel'. The above-mentioned Thomas Mellon Benedict had his experience with a 'being of light' who was not a past close relative or friend and strangely, when conversing with Benedict, informed him that "Human beings where given the power to heal themselves before the beginning of the world".

Mr Benedict had his experience on the operating table and was pronounced 'clinically dead' for one and a half hours. Surely very few, if any, doctors could accept that the brain would not be permanently brain damaged after such a period of time. Nevertheless, Mr Benedict not only came back with all his faculties intact after this lengthy period of oxygen starvation, he was cured of terminal cancer.

These events are startling enough but when we analyse the words of 'The Being of Light' as I said in *The Human Enigma*, it appears to support the theory rather strongly, that the human brain contains currently unidentified material (making up most of the mass of the brain) that could have been donated by 'beings of light', A.K.A. ET'S long ago and maybe capable of wondrous achievements in times to come, why else would it be there? Natural selection and evolution never endows any creature in advance of its needs to survive, but humans have this power, to be able to cure any human malady. We have said that downbeat, morose individuals constantly worrying over their health problems, are more likely to produce symptoms of ill health in themselves, but on the other hand a positively thinking person dwelling on other issues than themselves. The opposite maybe true.

This could imply that the cures at Lourdes for example, where some are cured (but not others) that they have been put down to the religious faith, may well be that the human brain acts in accordance with the positive signals given out strongly by the electrical forces within the human power pack. This is implied in the expression 'Faith can move mountains'. But to return to the subject of death of the irreversible kind, medical science has set its parameters, but they see, in some cases, to be quite conservative in their estimates, when stating in terms of hours, with regard to the 'point of no return', i.e. irreparable damage, but these times are not set in stone and medical science will admit that there are always exceptional circumstances this was certainly the case with Mr Benedict, but there was much more to it than simply defying the brain death issue. With Mr Benedict having returned with his terminal cancer cured.

To return to the N.D.E. issue, the body sometimes temporarily has (to use modern parlance) 'given up the ghost'. There is of course, clinical death, brain death and the biological termination of the body.

In the book *Human Development* by (Brown and Benchmar) it states "Death of the brain occurs when it fails to receive a sufficient supply of oxygen for a short period of time, usually eight to ten minutes??? The cessation of brain function occurs in three stages, first the cortex stops, then the mid-brain fails, and finally the brain stem ceases to function. When all these things occur brain death is completed". Yet, clearly, in some cases, as already mentioned, they all appear to be completely defied.

However, to continue with the article, "When all these factors are completed, the result is said to be an irreversible coma". This is the condition that causes so much grief and heartache, when at some point, where the grieving relatives, who eventually have to make the heart rending decision whether or not to terminate the life support functions. It is even more disturbing for them when they have previously heard of cases, where, just before the final decision was made, the subject miraculously recovers, defying all the expected processes, in particular, defying the formerly agreed upon definitions of brain death. The estimate mentioned in the book (quoted) of eight to ten minutes for the onset of brain death, does indeed seem to be very conservative, when Greek sponge divers for example can stop breathing for at least half or more of that time, and indeed, some illusionists, in tricks involving themselves being submerged in water, have seriously approached the completion of this amount or time, where there was no question that they were holding their breath.

In the early part of the twentieth century Harry Houdini was quite proficient in this type of illusion, but perhaps 'illusion' is the wrong word, the act is plain to see and as much as we may not like to admit it, people enjoy watching others courting death, which is why the Formula One race meetings were so well attended before it became safer than driving on the M1.

Houdini was aware, that if he did not get everything just right, he may meet his end. He is documented as having an avid interest in the possibility of an afterlife added to this, was his love for his mother and whether he may see her again in the form of another realm of existence. In this, he attended many spiritual séances and exposed many fraudulent mediums along the way, as spiritualism was very popular in those times. Nowadays, we approach the realms of spirituality in a more 'picky' or scientifically orientated way and need firm convincing, yet serious debate of the issue still prevails, as everyone has a vested interest in what will eventually happen to them.

Religious belief has to be a factor in this issue; due to the often-repeated statement of the warm loving experience encounter encompassing them which some have interpreted as 'heavenly'. An interesting quote from a recovering alcoholic was given in the aforementioned book *Human Development*, who stated, "Religion is for those who are afraid to go to hell; spirituality is a revival for those who have already been there".

Although Harry Houdini wanted, as said, to believe in an afterlife, he was frequently angry and frustrated when encountering so many frauds. It was a flourishing money making enterprise by people who exploited gullible humans and their genuine feelings and belief in the afterlife.

However, not all of these mediums appeared fraudulent and did not always use their talents for monetary gain. These occurrences made Houdini pay more attention to the issue. These kinds of people are sometimes held in high regard and often have to travel when being invited to display their gifts at various venues and must require some form of reimbursement. So one would not begrudge them a fee or an entry charge to their show.

The usual wish and theme of their display is to try to convince others that they need not despair and that their electrical energy or 'aura' cannot be extinguished by death but simply manifests itself in a different form. Again, the most appropriate name for it must be the 'soul'. Nevertheless, the brain has a healthy curiosity, in one example, a well known medium in front of an audience handled personal items brought by the audience and after holding it for a while would eventually identify the person who had brought in the item and would then go about the business of identifying the person who had passed it on, which may be a deceased relative or close friend. This sometimes invoked strong emotional effects in the audience and in particular, displayed in the person who had brought the item, showing sadness and happiness in equal proportions, certainly, when the medium seemed to get it right with the description of the person who had previously owned the item.

Obviously, this would confirm to the living person in the audience that there is an afterlife and that their relative still lived on in a different realm of existence.

The convinced member in the audience asked, "Where is Aunty Bessie now?" the medium replies, "She is right here beside me and she is holding a bunch of flowers she picked from her own garden".

At that point, we could stop and consider what a more cynical and questioning person would start to think and evaluate what was happening before him. Let us put the medium in an imaginary witness box in a court of law, with a clever barrister subjecting the medium to some sort of cross-examination process.

"You say this person from the afterlife picked a bunch of flowers from her own garden" (reply unknown), "Well ..... a garden naturally implies her garden was part of her house, are there other houses there? If so this implies she, in some way, acquired a house when she passed over, could you explain how?" (reply unknown) "Are there Estate Agents in the town? After all if there are other houses, there must be roads and some kind of urban area, a village, or a town perhaps? Is there any traffic moving about? Other people beside Aunt Bessie must also exist; does the town or area have a name?" (reply unknown) "If she picked the flowers from her own garden we must assume there were no weeds or wild flowers and she grew them from seeds, are there any garden centers nearby where she could have bought the seeds? (reply unknown). "Did she walk to the garden centre or the town, or are there buses and taxis there? Or did she somehow float there in some kind of spiritual form?

These sort of questions could be seen as flippant and uncaring that could upset the person who was convinced that the medium was actually in some kind of spiritual contact with the loved one but they are the kind of questions that could be asked by someone who plainly 'just does not buy it'.

Humans do have these questioning abilities which prevent people having 'blind faith' which is said to be a pre-requisite to accept certain parts of the Biblical genesis, yet in many people, ardent belief does appear to override uncomfortable alternative theories.

Some, in response may say, that we should not expect things in the afterlife to be a mirror image of how we existed on Earth, but that could not really be accepted as an alternative explanation as it explains nothing and is more akin to an avoidance of any kind of analysis of the subject.

In setting up this imaginary scenario, it can only be seen as facetious or uncaring, but they are definitely the type of questions that some self-important 'Philadelphia Lawyer' might well ask, in attempting to make some logic of things accepted as spiritual.

My own personal near death experience occurred, not on an operating table but in a hot fly infested zone in South Yemen, where a bullet with my name on it swished past my ear so closely that the air that it pushed in front of it actually caused my earlobe to move slightly and that is as close as I ever wish to be, to a near death experience. However, I am comfortable with the conception of an afterlife and like many people, hope it is so. It usually takes one to experience an event for oneself that seems to fall into the category of the unexplained. Most people in later life can recall an incident in their life that they wish they could explain in logical terms and I am no exception.

My father died relatively young from peritonitis, which, I am sure he would admit was largely self-inflicted not being a chap who would visit a doctor after every 'twinge', and also having experienced problems with stomach ulcers he would simply state to my stepmother "I'll take a bit of bi-carb".

Sadly he did not recover and when the funeral arrangements were made I was happy to be asked to be a pallbearer. It was the height of winter when my wife, children and I set off for Barrow-in-Furness, snow was falling heavily and I passed the snow-covered sign for Ulverston and finished in Penrith.

When I finally reached my stepmother's house, I noticed in my peripheral vision on my right, in the front room window, a figure half rise as though enquiring who was arriving. I assumed it was one of my late father's friends who had come to comfort my stepmother. After we had got the children and baggage inside, my stepmother must have wondered why I kept looking at the front room door, I was expecting someone to emerge. Finally, I asked her "Who is in the front room?" My stepmother looked a little wide-eyed at this and replied "No one". Later, it turned out that my father's favourite chair was by the front room window.

Naturally this and most experiences can be explained away by people offering alternative explanations, such as "Oh, it was just your own reflection in the glass". I would not hire a lawyer to argue against it but I know my movements did not synchronise with the figure's movement in the front room window.

There is another strange situation to dwell on, when one passes on and presumably meets up in the warm kindly light and meets up with one's deceased relatives, how would it be, to be hugging your late father who was twenty years younger than you? What happens with the ageing process? Does it remain static? If it continues what then? One cannot die twice.

It has been suggested, that the N.D.E. experience of the 'tunnel' is the brains last gasp and winds itself back to the beginning of its experiences. The 'tunnel' being the birth canal and the warm light is the neon lights of the operating room, figures all around smiling, wrapping the newly born in a warm blanket and so forth. Then you are placed into the arms of a loving person stroking your face and cooing over you.

Of course, this kind of imaginative scene would be shattered, if you where hung up by the heels and received a resounding smack across the buttocks designed to clear your breathing passages of mucus as the crying started. One assumes this practice has been discontinued, if it was ever necessary in the first place.

The subject of reincarnation must also come into the picture; it is a well-enriched belief in some countries, India, for example. The soul now free from the body, is somehow able to enter a new body getting another chance, as it were, to experience another life. The first thing we would ask would be who would be deemed as qualifying for this 'honour', or is it a punishment? As the daily volume of souls flooding into the judgement hall, who decides who will go into another body and become active at the first heartbeat of the foetus?

Some of those who have experienced an N.D.E. felt somehow 'disappointed' at having returned into their body. Surely, such a person assuming, that they had a choice, would not wish to go into a strange body, but stay in the warm loving light.

If one had been a particularly nasty or evil being in their life, they would have no business expecting another chance and would surely be assigned to one of the places we mentioned, either an extremely long stay in limbo being a 'purged' of their evil or the other type, being made to reflect on their evil deed forever. They would be happy to go into another body if they got the chance.

As for the righteous ones who had led a chaste and unblemished life, they would get what they were promised during the Sermon on the Mount by Jesus himself, "Blessed are the pure in heart, for they shall see God". So, who is left to enter a new body? And how does the new body feel about it? It had worked away for nine months converting a mass of cells into the double helix D.N.A. chromosomes and so forth for its new body that it will soon expel, why should it have someone else's second hand soul imposed on it?

If it really happens, why cannot the forces that 'arranged' for it to happen, that the reincarnated soul starts afresh, with all previous memories erased? However, this is not the case. Extreme confusion, often sadness and upset prevails as the reincarnated soul starts to relive its memories. A child starts relating things that it could not have known and becomes sometimes quite disturbed about it. Often upsetting the mother by coldly stating "You're not my real mother" and this, after she had gone through all the discomfort for some nine months and then had to bear the pain of the birth process, just to be told that she is not the mother of the child, this would be most upsetting.

Both male and female children have provided a host of details regarding the way they died. An air crash, train crash, a fire or car crash etc., and in most cases, the parents out of either just curiosity or a definite need to know, follow up on all the information provided by the child and it usually checks out and appears to be correct.

Sometimes (at no small expense) they may take the child, sometimes to another country and the child will point out the scenes they had previously described sometimes in great detail.

Clearly, if all the data checks out and the parents are perfectly sure that they had never taken their child to these specific locations, then they would have little choice other than to accept it and consider the subject of reincarnation to be factual. What do they do then? Who would envy anyone in that position?

But we have to ask, is it fair that the unidentified power should put the child and its parents through such an ordeal? The child in these cases does not seem evil or nasty, so why did it not just progress in the spirit world? The being that was responsible for the act, must be accountable for the stress and the suffering of both the child and the parents, of course, rationality must always prevail and remains as an alternative consideration in these cases and logical explanations are always sought. To explain them for example, the child has read a story or an exciting young adventure of an occurrence put together from scenes viewed on TV there are plenty of media outlets where such stories could be imprinted in the child's memory as said, television, a book from the school library and so forth but rationality should not debar any possibility of the phenomena being genuine, simply because it appears as irrational.

One would expect that if this great power decides to designate the soul of a deceased person to a newborn, then this same power ought surely, to wipe the slate clean, regarding the previous owner's life experiences, rather than put the child and the parents through all the aforementioned disturbances, the recipients deserved the chance to live and attain its own experiences rather than to relive somebody else's.

The human brain is a fragile and sensitive organ and many things still need to be explained regarding its workings. Different parts of the unborn infant's brain develops at different rates, so must the cognitive factors and, as in the above cases, the sense later, of not being entirely oneself. It is a matter of record (as we have said) that the mother of a child notices that all is not quite right with the child and have even expressed the feeling that the child is not completely hers. We have previously said also, the child itself sometimes looks quizzically at the mother in such a way that the child appears to be saying, "Who are you? I don't recognise you". And this marks the onset of the situation above beginning to develop. The following may sound like something straight out of the X Files, that is because it is. I can only ever recall watching one episode of the series, which was good (entertainment wise) this was not because I did not like the series, but because it usually clashed with something else, I preferred to watch. The series ran for some time and dealt with most things paranormal.

One programme dealt with the subject of reincarnation. Howard Gordon, the writer of the series, was rather cynical with his remark "Everyone in their past life was either a chieftain or a princess". No one ever claimed to be a dishwasher.

I found this remark quite interesting, the reason for this will become apparent. The above remark caused me to recall an interesting event when younger, that we purposely brought about, but seemed to mirror the statement by Howard Gordon. Most people during their lifetime, particularly when young, do many things either for bravado or out of simple curiosity or just through interest, that older and wiser adults advise against.

However, this did not deter my mother-in-law (who had a sense of fun) from taking part, along with my wife and I, including my brother-in-law, in a contrived session with an Ouija board, we looked at it as simply a bit of fun. My brother-in-law was quite reluctant to become involved, even though he was a lot younger than we were. So, he took on the much safer task of standing aside and simply taking notes, in case we did manage to contact someone from the afterlife. When we began, I found it quite remarkable when we all put our fingers on the glass, how a distinct feeling of a kind of vibration energy as though that glass was rearing to go.

We did not use a 'bought item' for the board with a planchette but rather placed cards with numbers and letters on a circular coffee table. After the customary "is there anybody there", the glass shot immediately to the first letter of a name which was David (someone), I cannot recall the second name but we naturally asked "who where you?"

At this point, we would mention the contrast between Howard Gordon's statement and the reply from, what we assumed was a now deceased spirit entity. We asked what he did in life and the rather surprising reply was that he was a refuse collector and that he had lived in Devon. He gave out some other details and indicated that he would look out for us in our life etc. I found this a bit worrisome, not wanting a spirit to be hanging around watching our every move. However, I (sometime after) asked my brother-in-law if he might have retained his notes but he had discarded them. I regret, with hindsight not having checked out the substantial amount of data, this David fellow provided. We used to be fond of visiting Devon and Cornwall and would have checked it out simply out of curiosity but did not consider what our reactions would have been if the data proved correct. In spite of what the 'wise ones' warned against, we pursued the business with the board and this time Howard Gordon turned to be partly right as the 'spirit' remarked that in a former existence I was a Highland Chieftain.

The experts in the field make it clear, that unless going through a series of precautionary measures such as paranormal investigations groups are said to do, one should not attempt to dabble in things one does not understand (we could ask, how else would we get to understand it?). Nevertheless, when one is young, one does not worry about such things, but the main danger is that it is said to be possible to invite a demonic entity into your life. Demons seem to fit into the same classification as the outmoded 'horned devil', but they could equally be souls who where despicably evil in life and are equally happy be just as evil in spirit form and would happily contaminate living beings, given the chance. These types of entities are said to be abject liars and would flatter you with their lies to gain your confidence and possibly an ultimate possession of your body. With regard to our dabbling with the Ouija board, my mother-in-law had recently lost her husband and specifically asked if he was there and to our surprise 'Norman', as he was called, came through. The replies to the questions are quite vague for the most part and one does not learn much from the spirit regarding the afterlife.

However, our little adventure with this form of entertainment came to an abrupt end by my wife who removed her finger from the glass rather abruptly that seemed to sever the contact with 'Norman' her stepfather. The reason for this was, that when my mother-in-law asked the question "What are you doing now?" The reply was, "Waiting for ....." and at that point, the contact was terminated. My wife assumed the last word would be 'you', referring to my mother-in-law.

We did not involve ourselves in anything of the kind again, but if the spirit was 'Norman' (my father-in-law); his waiting is over, because now she (my mother-in-law) is with him. It would appear that some people have got themselves so involved with this type of contact (having ignored all the advice) that they have virtually allowed it to rule their lives. Also, that if a demonic entity can enter your body the only way it can be removed would be to be expelled by an exorcism .

With regard to reincarnation, Howard Gordon's view is that the evidence for it is so scant, but many would argue against that in view of the number of cases we have previously described and also (one may suppose) the entire population of India.

The most high profile case regarding the subject of reincarnation was the highly publicised story of Bridey Murphy, that at one point, was (one might say) 'the talk of the town'. It is not so well known today (and some people say it was all a hoax anyway), but 'fate' magazine in the USA that dealt with the stories of the strange and unknown , apparently ran an article in their November 1956 issue titled 'Bridey Murphy in Ireland'. It was the results of a personal investigation by William J Barker.

In the same year, a book was published, written by a Colorado hypnotherapist named Morey Bernstein. This gentleman had conducted hypnotherapy sessions with a certain Virginia Tighe. This lady was returned to a past life that she had supposedly lived in nineteenth century Ireland.

It turned out, that in her trancelike state, she took on a different character and even conversed using a thick Irish brogue. Although she seemed, either a very good actress or quite convincing, not everything she said could be proven beyond any doubt as absolutely accurate. She had named such people who where the local villagers rather convincingly, as though she had actually known them. Among these people, that if she had in fact, lived before in that village she would naturally have come into contact with them. Among them where priests, grocers, and other shopkeepers, who (along with all the other villagers) she would have known and in fact did prove to be correct.

However, it was stated that none of this proves that Mrs Tighe could have come by all this information by other means. In the Bridey Murphy case a youth Shawnee Oklahoma, was so affected by the story in the aforesaid book, that was widely read, in fact had become a best seller, that he was said to have committed suicide and was said to have left a message that read "They say curiosity killed

STRANGE REALITIES

the cat, well I'm curious about this Bridey Murphy, I'm going into the afterlife in order to investigate it personally".

It seems quite amazing that someone could be so badly affected by a story in a book that they would go so far as to take their own life, as interesting as it may be, what was so important that made him so desperate to prove it?"

The idea of reincarnation is not a new concept by any means and goes back into history for millennia, indeed, it is the basic tenet of some of the world religions but rarely deals with deeper questions regarding the whys and wherefores, but simply accepts it. Such a subject as reincarnation, must take its place in the field of the paranormal, but as is the case with many other subjects, rarely comes to any positive conclusions and discussions regarding these topics that always revolve in circles with no firm conclusions being reached. If reincarnation becomes an established fact, then it would certainly implicate the existence of the 'soul' or a spiritual being but all such topics always remain the subject of philosophical debate. It is said that no 'bits', inputs or items of information are lost and forgotten, that enter the human brain and that anyone who is proficient in such matters only has to press the right button or strike the right cord to contact the brains cellular computerised memory banks to elicit or bring forth the required information that is forever logged therein.

There is a name given that explains this ability of the human brain, that encompasses and absorbs everything that we see, smell, touch hear, see and taste and that is 'cryptomnesia' (literally hidden memory).

A good example of this ability to bring forth the necessary data, could be, utilised during a court hearing or a police case. A witness for instance, who only vaguely remembers seeing a certain vehicle at or near the scene of the crime, would be of little use in obtaining a conviction, with such absence of detail, but on the other hand, if the witness agreed to, or was put under hypnosis, often, quite amazingly the brain comes up with the necessary information and the hypnotised witness can even recall, not only the correct make and model of the vehicle, but the colour and the licence plate number, proving that the brain captures everything down to the last detail.

Of course, all these events and occurrences make for healthy debate in which rationality prevails and a more logical reason is sought to explain what seem to be paranormal issues. ESP, ghosts,. UFOs, levitation, pre-cognition, all of these factors fall under the label of the paranormal, but in times to come, with possibly increased brain development of its currently dormant areas, these topics may have to be classified as 'normal'.

Of course, everything regarding these matters and many revelations possibly still to come, come under control of the most mystifying organ in the human body, namely, the human brain.

Occasionally, paranormal and ecclesiastical events are hard to separate and categorise. Miracles, for example, often result in canonisation to the priesthood, but again, they could be another example of the brain's currently hidden capabilities.

Anyone with just a modicum of curiosity cannot help but be interested in the currently unexplainable and this is certainly borne out by the viewing figures of TV programmes that deal with these issues and are once more in vogue (the Von Däniken Legacy).

The X Files, ghosts, haunted houses, poltergeist activity, many paranormal investigation groups have arisen in recent years that are attempting to get some answers and do sometimes produce some interesting results. Just as Professor J Allen Hynek said with regard to the UFO phenomena, that serious investigation is sullied by the 'kooks and nuts' with fraudulent trickery, so are the serious paranormal investigators with the advent of modern computer technology and hidden cameras, they can duplicate many of the events under the paranormal label. With regard to these tricks, it is noticeable that the events are always in full view of the camera not behind it or to the side, which surely tells us something.

With regard to the UFO phenomena, it seems to be one of the easiest factors of the unexplained to duplicate, and has been, ever since the first car hubcap was thrown and photographed. J Allen Hynek, the guru of UFO investigations, highlighted this issue of fraud, he made it clear that the UFO phenomena is real and certainly, the huge amount of cases he has personally investigated, saw his actual conversion from renowned sceptic to believer, points out that the phenomena is a real puzzle and "The subject has not been 'put to rest', and we must now recognise that we can no longer dismiss the subject in the usual ways, I say this from the start so that you are not misled by the kooks, the nuts and the gullible, which has made this subject so hard to study rationally?

As we have said, this also applies to the other aspects of the paranormal. Of course, investigation groups, which seriously approach the subject with quite sophisticated detection equipments, such as so-called 'spirit boxes' and 'motion detectors', that alight up if a form of spiritual energy approaches it, do get positive results.

One particular investigation took place in the home of a lady who was experiencing psychic type of phenomena mainly directed toward her children and as I have already stated I experienced this myself (not directly) but in accounts later related to my sons when we stayed at the home of my stepmother in Barrow-in-Furness for my father's funeral. To return to the case above, the lady began to sense that it may be her mother that was trying to contact her. She confided with the group by revealing a special word that the lady and her mother had agreed upon should it ever be possible to make contact from the afterlife.

The investigating group, together with their specialist equipment were able to receive a 'voice', that the lady immediately recognised as that of her late mother, but more profoundly, the special word known only to the lady and her mother clearly came through.

The lady was obviously quite shocked and was reduced to an emotional state. The programme and the participant came across as genuine. Although it seems highly unlikely, we have no way of knowing, if the whole show had been purposely contrived embellished or modified for that dramatic effect. As we have said, anything can be faked or set up beforehand by anyone wishing to portray a situation as genuine.

However, this would be unfair to the media or the programme makers, they have a controlling code of ethics, and there are 'whistle blowers'. Large crews are employed to make the programmes, someone could 'talk', it is unlikely that they would risk their business in such a way, but it is a different story when people setting out to hoax people and use the internet to do so.

People like to be intrigued, that is why the 'world domination' theme is so popular with the superhero who comes to the fore to put a stop to it. Conspiracy theories abound, TV programmes are made where a sinister high-powered group of mega rich people, scientists, bankers, top politicians and so forth control everything that goes on in the world, in other words, they rule it, and control humanity.

They consider the depletion of the natural resources, possible food shortages and famine. They view it as a very serious matter that the world's population expansion is getting out of hand and consider methods of 'culling' humanities numbers, even purposely introducing viruses into the population throughout the world, having taken steps, of course, to protect themselves.

They are aware of the thin veneer of civilisation is with regard to the masses, who so easily resort to anarchistic behaviour, who prefer to destroy rather than offer anything better and are quickly able to descend into a rioting destructive mob. We see it all too often on our television sets.

They meet to discuss how to handle a situation where such behaviour spreads worldwide. It is entirely possible, that right now a programme in the conspiracy theory vein is even now being made stating that the current pandemic of corona virus was purposely introduced into the world population for the aforesaid reasons.

People like to be shocked and given all these topics to dwell on. It is big business for the film and TV producers, but that is life. The UFO theorists may already be thinking on similar lines and that is ET's who are responsible for human disasters, the reduction of the ozone layer and so forth.

Of course, there may be a perfectly natural explanation for pandemics. The Spanish flu, rampant in 1918, killed millions and an explanation by astronomers Fred Hoyle and Chandra Wickerman Singh was offered or should we say 'theory', that is came from space, that is from cometary tails of the past, where the Earth passes through them on its travels around the Sun. the dust sprinkles down onto the Earth as the tiny particles stream into our atmosphere, which is also augmented by the daily dose of meteoric dust that arrives on Earth from burned out meteors every day. This is not an unreasonable proposition. This ingrained fear in the human psyche is why these 'holocausts' and conspiracy theories abound. This fear of the unknown is the cause of our 'shoot first ask questions later' mindset. It manifests itself in the UFO phenomena, where frequent aggressive attacks on unknown objects in the sky by fighter jets or laser attacks from the ground often occur, yet fortunately this alleged higher power does not respond (luckily for us) in like manner.

Humans tend to view certain things they do not understand as a threat. This has been with us since our ancient tribal days of the past. There is no doubt that the UFO phenomena is real, it is the correct interpretation of it that is important.

If it is an advanced extra terrestrial visitation, then such an advancement that does not threaten Earth (entirely due to the length of time it has prevailed). Why then attack it? It if it so advanced, clearly it would become a threat to us if we continuously provoke it. It cannot help but display this advanced technology as it manifests itself in our skies and of course the many encounters of the various kinds. It cannot 'hide' its technology.

Humans long into the future (if we have one) will most probably display our own technology to a possible less advanced race on another world somewhere in the cosmos. We certainly would not expect to be attacked for it, but rather 'revered' by the natives just as the Biblical characters did when advanced beings descended on their 'pillars of fire' in front of the patriarchs. Even our own sciences cause fear among the masses who do not understand the technology behind them, but having said that, even the scientists on the 'Manhattan Project' such as Robert Oppenheimer who feared what they were creating. The C.E.R.N Project is a good example where a handful of boffins could, for all we know easily be putting the rest of us in great danger, simply due to their insatiable 'need to know' and thereby closing their minds to any possible danger, or by (it is suggested) playing 'God' by searching for the secrets of creation and tampering with natures dangerous forces. They have already admitted that they are trying to create a 'black hole' but of course, it will only be a little one and it is nothing for us to worry about (famous last words), however, that is another issue.

If we return to the subject of the spirit and the afterlife. The interest prevails, simply because of the compelling wish, to believe that death is not the end of things and that their loved ones have passed onto a better existence, free of the pressure, pain and strife often experienced in real life that they might have had to bear when alive.

This is of course, why the paranormal programmes and investigative groups, spiritualists and so forth exist. They fill in modern parlance) 'a gap in the market'. We have dealt with the dangers of untrained individuals out of sheer curiosity or fun filled diversions, involving themselves in the use of Ouija boards and so forth and the dangers of inviting evil into their lives.

Demonologists tell us that since saintly people and profound good exists, it follows that there is an opposite force we describe as evil. When the saintly individuals pass on they are said to get their just desserts by being able to enter a higher plain we call 'heaven', but the thoroughly evil people are terrified of being judged and 'cast down' as they may believe will happen, and as a result, are content to remain in the earthly realm and would never 'go into the light'. Therefore, they are happy to continue to revel in their evil and stride the Earth seeking the ruination of souls. If such beings do exist in the afterlife it would be natural to assume there is some kind of 'hierarchy' of the demons with the head of their number being designated as 'the prince of darkness', 'the devil' or whatever name we assign to it. This certainly makes sense if we are to believe in a divine infallible God. Everything has its equal and opposite force and there is said to be a hierarchy of 'angels'. If thoroughly evil people do live on in an ethereal existence, they would, as said, surely have to be under some kind of control, as their number is so vast, that contacts have been told, "We are legion". Such an entity may welcome a recently executed criminal after performing heinous deeds on Earth was a 'Sieg Heil' and say "Welcome to our group, I must tell you, when I was alive, I had great fun in sanctioning the murder of six million people, can you match that?" The evil new arrival then gets his assignment to ruin the souls of so many living people as possible. He maybe told "In particular be watchful of the people who try to make contact with those who have passed on and jump in whenever you get the chance, but be careful at first, with sweet words, until you know they can been brought under your influence".

Nevertheless, people do court such things as 'possession' unknowingly. None of this is too worrisome for young people who have this sense of invulnerability and that they are in full control of their lives. They may have approached the subject in a frivolous manner by the aforementioned curiosity, resulting in experiments with a Ouija board not realising that they are 'inviting' a spiritual entity to their lives, which is all the entity needs. On a lighter note, I will quote a sentence from a book dealing with the 'X Files', "Is there anybody there? if not, just say No". With regard to any of this, possibly, risky experimentation with unknown forces, 'just say no', clearly we are all uncertain, just as when the old lady was asked "Do you believe in ghosts?", replied "No of course not, But I'm still frightened of them". When we watch a DVD classic of an old film, we may be watching actors on the screen who have all passed away, we are looking at ghosts. The piece of electronic equipment allows us to show them. Another device in our hand allows us to show them over and over if we wish.

Ghostly sightings are repeated over and over on Earth where the phantom has passed on and we can no more contact him or her by interaction than we could by trying to grab the attention of one of the actors in our DVD film. The electronic envelope that encompasses the world, allows them to appear and reappear in the ether and causes the electronic forces in the human body and brain to activate and (but not all) to make the electronic connection that switches on the recording of their actions imprinted on the ether around the globe for humans to view.

When I said "Not all", the electronic forces in the human brain allows some individuals to switch on and view the apparitions but not all. The brain is 'hardwired' differently in some individuals. A first class example is the brain of Einstein that has been preserved, sliced up and analysed. The intelligence services much prefer to employ people who do not think in 'straight lines' as it were. People that come to the same conclusions as the majority, simply because the conclusion seems logical. This is sometimes evident in people who frequently use the word 'they'. For example, if asked for their opinion on a well-debated subject, the person may respond by saying "Well …. 'they' say that so and so is the answer. A better response would perk up the interest of an interviewer, if the response was, its generally believed that the answer could be so and so but I don't buy that, personally, I think …." Therefore, not thinking in straight lines by being more analytical and questioning.

To return to ghostly apparitions, cases are on record (but not necessarily on film) for example of a Roman soldier walking, not on the ground that the witness perceives, but slightly above it, in other words, the ground as it was in the soldiers time. Chester was once heavily occupied by the Romans and this type of story emerges in the so-called ghost walks that most of the historic towns have on offer; it may even be shown that historically that is where a sentry would be patrolling.

Again, alleged actual footage of ghosts are swamped in the deluge of fake depictions that can so easily be contrived today, which, as we have said, makes it so difficult to separate the 'wheat from the chaff' as it were. This also exists in the UFO phenomena.

The subject of spirits, however, is a different matter. They are separated in many ways from ghosts. Spirits are a form of energy and not 'depictions'. Nevertheless, 'images' have been recorded on film that interact in some way with investigative teams. The essential difference between them and ghosts is this interaction. They can often be assisted in the incantation largely encouraging them to 'go to the light'. What is this 'light', what is its source? We may never know until we are moving into it ourselves. We may not be meant to know. The strongest form of spiritual energy i.e. 'poltergeist' activity may not be from a spirit at all, as it is suggested to be 'human' energy and the results manifested are from the person it mostly interacts with, usually an adolescent, but often the manifestations occur when the person is not present, for example, a pile of chairs stacked in a way that would be hardly possible to construct by hand, and are re-seen when returning to the house. Clearly, ghosts and spirits are big business, why else would we have so many paranormal investigative groups and media attention in the various TV programmes. With all the violence around us that exists today, some people say, "It's the living we should worry about, not the dead, they can't hurt you".

This is not strictly true and can be disputed. Many an operator of a paranormal investigation group has been physically harmed, usually in the form of scratches to the body, usually the back, often reacting with a yelp and other members of the team may lift the shirt of the 'victim' and find (usually three deep scratches often oozing blood. Again, how do we account for these events?

Of course, it may be offered, that the wounds are simply another form of 'stigmata' in that the investigator is apprehensive and having heard of similar attacks affecting previous investigators, is somehow 'expecting' it and the power of the mind (which is a force to be reckoned with) does the rest.

Stigmata, in the form of replicating the wounds of Christ when crucified, have appeared on a holy person dwelling deeply on the anguish and the suffering of Jesus and then produces the wounds due to the mystical forces in the mind/brain.

We must ask do animals have a soul? Particularly dogs who, interact with humans so deeply. Special images in film footage do exist of dogs and cats assuming the footage is genuine.

In one particular case, a person who had two dogs lost one of them to cancer, which can afflict them as well as humans. Before it passed away, it had worn a collar containing small bells woven into the materials and because of this, the family always knew it was around and where it was. Shortly after it died, the soft jingling of bells was heard. The other dog would react quite noticeably, would lower its head and with its front paws spread out, would adopt the stance that it did, when about to play with the other dog. That is when it was about to jump forward and it was seen staring at the point where the jingling noise was coming from.

The belief in the existence of the spirit in humans as they pass on, should in theory, encourage those still alive toward good behaviour while on Earth, because clearly, if they do pass on in spirit they would expect to be 'judged' and would surely wish to present themselves as having been a good person, rather than a more dark unsavoury character. In addition, one assumes they would be happier to 'go to the light' rather than to remain hanging about on Earth.

However, many spirits must have found themselves in this situation or else all the paranormal groups would have no 'trade'. Invariably they are encouraged to go into the light and seem happy to do so.

A crafty person in life may still be equally crafty in the afterlife. If somehow they find themselves unwillingly trapped on Earth, they may simply head for the nearest house and haunt to their hearts content, while knowing that the occupants will eventually call in an investigative team that will help them. As a result, when commanded, the spirit will scamper off into the light. Alternatively, thoroughly evil entities, when they pass on, such as murderers, hit men and other evil doers that where so deep in blood, would feel that they would have no hope of going 'into the light', indeed, they would be terrified to do so.

If they escape the kind of hell that is depicted in tradition and religious beliefs, and they are going to be trapped on Earth forever, they would be happy to follow the evil path and join the legion of the damned. They would be even more delighted to jump into a body and possess it, if invited perhaps by a group fooling around with an Ouija board.

They would logically pick out whom they perceived as the weakest being who may not have the strength of character to resist their manipulations that would certainly include flattery and a pretence of help. Whereas exorcism was fairly common in the past, the Catholic Church is somewhat reluctant to condone them today and tend to agree with the medical viewpoint, that the malady in the person suspects of being 'possessed' is purely a mental issue, where the brain has forced this belief into the subject. However, in some cases, it may agree to one, on a 'nothing to lose' basis, if mental therapy has failed. It seems that for the most part this chore falls to the Jesuit. One assumes from this, that as part of their ecclesiastical studies they are specifically trained in the practice. It is usually portrayed, in films particularly, that the process entails much danger to the person carrying out the procedure. This would make sense as mental home staff confront this problem as par for the course in their establishments.

However, to return to the subject of general paranormal activity, the experiences can be felt by anyone at anytime regardless of the location, especially with regard to ghostly apparitions.

It seems to be a feature of ghostly apparitions, that they occur when one least expects it. Perhaps this is due to the equilibrium of the mind when in a more relaxed mode and the electronic circuits of the brain are more receptive.

The opposite may be the case when one purposely visits a stately home or castle, keyed up and expectant, where a different set of mental circuits are involved and as a result may see nothing, but a more relaxed member of staff, humming away to themselves, going about their assistant chores may suddenly be confronted with a clear cut and obvious apparition.

A onetime Politician called Jeremy Thorpe, was invited to dinner with friends in a large location, when moving through a different part of the house, he relates that he came close to what he thought was a real person, so much so, that he bid it good day. When he conferred later with the others, they were not surprised and were used to the ghostly presence and that he was known as the 'prior'. This case is interesting in the sense of what we have discussed regarding the condition of the brain at a certain time. If Jeremy Thorpe had known about the 'prior' in advance, he would have been looking about expectantly and therefore would probably have seen nothing. When we discussed the, what could called, 'pre-requisites' in order to attain the heavenly abode after we have passed on, why would a rich person be automatically barred from entering the heavenly abode? After all, the words of Jesus himself stated, "A rich man has as much chance of entering the Kingdom as a camel would of passing through the eye of a needle". The person may have inherited the wealth, perhaps as an only son and heir. He may be a good person and be contributing to many charities and worthy causes.

Surely, such a statement would be better applied to the evil doers on Earth and not someone who is rich by inheritance, implying that being rich is comparable to a crime. Rich people generate wealth by employment perhaps of many others. They also, (apart from those who scurry off to tax havens) contribute largely to the Government coffers in order that they can carry out their social programmes. Surely rich employers are more worthy than those who are so streetwise that they know all the tricks of obtaining as much in benefits as they can and avoid work at all costs, taking state handouts and contributing nothing to the state.

To return to paranormal issues all members of an investigative team no doubt have a mixture of widely experienced members and other more recently joined members. They, no doubt, have a few shocks to bear, along the way toward becoming experienced. This was highlighted in one case, where a team found themselves at an allegedly haunted venue. One member of the team was quite sceptical and this is no bad thing.

It would seem to be good practice to have someone who would question an occurrence and look for a logical explanation rather than simply going along with the likelihood that it is spiritual and then go on to accept every creak, groan and murmur, as paranormal when this is a common feature of old empty buildings and may also be attributed to outside weather conditions.

During the investigation, this new member looked up and encountered the figure of a girl standing in front of him, thinking that she also was a new member of the team; he began to speak to her, when she just faded away, as no doubt would his sceptism as the event shook him up noticeably.

A rather disturbing aspect of this whole paranormal issue would be to find that the spirits of the dead could have control over who lives and dies on Earth, but that is what the following account in a sense, does imply. It involves an actual occurrence, in the wake of an air crash and they became what is called 'protective ghosts', but to 'protect' one must have some kind of 'power'. They would be more aptly called 'protective spirits', but they would qualify as ghosts as their image has been seen by many people, but the major difference is that they do react to the living. These two people were employed by Eastern Airlines in the US and they have been seen by other flight crews of the same airline and even a President of Eastern Airlines. One of the dead aircrew was sitting in a seat that was next to that of an elderly lady, he was in his uniform and appeared as alive as anyone else, when he simply disappeared, throwing the lady into hysterics.

This same ghostly apparition interacted with the flight crew and told them "Watch out for the fire on this airplane" The galley area. One captain, working for the same airline, was told "There will never be another crash involving this type of aircraft"...... "We will not let it happen", and indeed no incident did occur, involving the aircraft in which the two aircrew died in, from December 1972 through 'till 1995 when this story was investigated.

We must analyse more deeply, the statement underlined above. These spirits, the two aircrew referred to as 'we', must, with such a statement, have the power to save lives, or, if they withdrew this power or did not exercise it, causalities or deaths would occur in other words, they have the power over life and death of the passengers travelling on that airline. Would they have the same power over the fate of passengers travelling on other airlines? What is the difference between allowing deaths to happen or causing them in terms of the law?

However, we must go onto analyse an even more disturbing consideration. If the spirits of the two-deceased aircrew have this power, why would they only be possessed of this power? What about the multitude of other spirits, still tied to the earthly realm, some of which may have been positively evil during their earthly lives? They would be delighted to have such power and could get even with hated enemies from beyond the grave.

It would be far more calming to the mind to review these cases as simply "interesting, well at least it proves there is life after death" and think no further. The statement by the two aircrew clearly implies that spirits can have power, but why did it take their deaths to gain the power? Did they have it when alive and not realise it?

Of course, there are cases involving not only aircraft and associated incidents, but maritime accounts involving spirits. Mariners are said to be the most superstitions, possibly with good reason, when we consider the following event. There is an account by Laura Kyte, regarding the seagoing liner named 'The Great Eastern', the vessel was plagued by a run of bad luck and strange occurrences such as the continually heard knocking sounds emanating from the hull. Eventually a skeleton was found of a hapless riveter, who had accidentally been entombed alive between the sheet metal plating's of the ships double hull.

One could imagine the reverts shouts and anguishing cries as he saw the giant sheet of metal suddenly extinguishing all the light as the crane maneuvered it into the place and the riveters crews, on bonus and time penalties, hurriedly beginning the riveting process. Shipyards are noisy places with steam hammers, drills, banging noises and foremen shouting orders and directives. The poor trapped riveter had no chance of attracting attention to his plight, but even after death, his hammering never stopped until his skeleton was found and his spirit freed.

There are a huge amount of factors that exist in the subject of life after death, ghosts, spirits, poltergeists and especially the unseen powers of the human brain, that are manifested in so many different ways. There are so many questions that require so many answers that do not seem to be forthcoming.

We have mentioned the pertinent factors that guide doctors, when going through the process of establishing clinical death, yet all these indications could and have been seen to be defied. It would surely be easier for a doctor to certify death after an unsuccessful attempt to save a life when on the operating table, surrounded by resuscitation equipment and other appliances plus the assistance of other colleagues, than another member of the medical profession. For example, an army surgeon of the medical corp., in the heat of battle, who has to decide if a soldier is dead or worth attempting to resuscitate. The decision has to be made quickly, for example, a stomach wound with internal bleeding. Dead bodies cannot be left lying around on the battle field any longer than necessary and there are said to be accounts emanating from the First World War, where bodies were temporarily interred in basic wooden boxes, designated to be exhumed later and re-buries respectfully in a military cemetery. Rather macabre stories have come to light where deep scratch marks with blood and tissue evident on the coffin lids above the body therein, where found when the temporary coffins where opened.

One assumes that all the required symptoms of life had been certified as 'extinguished', before the body was interred, so the only explanation possible would be a 'cataleptic trance', or severe coma brought on by the trauma of the battlefield producing all the symptoms of death. During the First World War, the casualties where enormous and military doctors would have been the busiest and most active of all the troops, with little time to devote to casualties, unlike a surgeon in a properly equipped hospital and has to prioritise and make quick decisions. 'Precognition' is another factor of this wide range of occurrences classified as paranormal, with its many facets, people bestowed with the ability of pre-cognition, would surely be more likely to view it as a curse rather than a gift, especially if it involved a person suddenly being able to foresee the death of a loved one. The subject involves a wide range of people who would not regard themselves as anyone special, even children have been bestowed with the ability. We may recall the horrific deaths of so many children in the Aberfan Disaster in Wales that occurred in 1966 where a slagheap collapsed after days of heavy rainfall loosened the pile. A first class example of an accident waiting to happen.

The pile cascaded down upon a school burying the children and teachers under a suffocating mass of slag. On the morning of October 20th when the tragedy occurred, a nine year old girl, Eryl Mai Jones, woke up from a nightmare and told her mum that she had gone to school that morning only to find that it was not there, "Because something black had come down all over it". Naturally, her mother would have comforted her saying it was just a dream. How many mothers would have kept their children away from school because of a dream?

Later, she dearly wished that she had, as the poor child died in the disaster. It must be said that a sizeable number of people have experienced such 'visions' or premonitions and heeded them, thereby saving their own life, cancelled flights, rail journeys, sea crossings and so forth have all been made because of such visions.

Strangely, a mathematician (William Cox) carried out a survey choosing rail accidents as his subject and found, when looking at passenger manifestos, that there were always fewer passengers on the ill-fated journey than on other trains of the same rail company. He found that their odds against this being a coincidence, extremely high. This would also seem to indicate just how many people have this exceptional ability. We may add, that the poor child mentioned predicting the Aberfan Disaster was not alone, a London psychiatrist Dr John Barker, investigated many of them and concluded that around sixty of them that came to light must be considered genuine. As a matter of fact, he was so impressed that he setup 'The British Premonitions Bureau', with the aim of perhaps of attempting to avert any future tragedies, but how difficult would it be to administer?

The people who may have had premonitions would surely have to be logged with their contact numbers the organisation would have to act quickly to set the wheels in motion. If a person contacted the Bureau and mentioned a flight that was due to takeoff that morning was in danger, the bureau would not have much success in convincing the airline to cancel the flight, with just one report. In the aviation industry, time in the air is profit, time on the ground is money lost, they could not be expected to run a business efficiently when responding to such information. A 'bomb scare' would be a different matter of course.

Neither would a rail company or a shipping company, comply for the same business reasons and could not run a business on 'hunches'. In order for such a bureau to operate efficiently, it would have to mount an expensive advertising and awareness programme with a well-publicised phone number, highlighted also on the TV networks. It would be rather like 'if you have a premonition, who you gonna call?"

This ability of pre-cognition is just another feature of the human brain and its capabilities, which have to decide if these articles where ever common place in this human brain or whether they are gradually developing, so that eventually, everyone will have them, there is a large portion of the human brain that is currently inactive but must surely develop otherwise what is the point in our having it? There are other strange features regarding the human brain. The human is akin to a powerful electrical device, more powerful in some, than others, that seem, to be able to tap into the similar energy field surrounding the Earth and make the necessary connections that cause poltergeist activity, for example, and even display the energy field by an aura seen by some (but no others) around the body.

The body seems able to store electrical energy like a powerful battery. There was a case in 1953 related in a magazine titled *Prediction*. It gave an account of a newborn child being delivered that gave the doctor delivering it, a noticeable jolt just as though he had touched a livewire. The child held this high voltage charge for twenty-four hours.

There was no mention of how, or if, the mother was in anyway affected but the doctor surely would have to explain very carefully to the mother why she could not hold her baby straightaway, I cannot see any way how he could. Perhaps she was told the child was being held for observation, however, the mother must have been rather stressed and worried until she finally held her child.

We have all seen shows that clearly indicate this electrical power, more evident in some than in others, where people are able to turn light bulbs on just by holding them between finger and thumb.

Strangely, these type of programmes usually result in people phoning in to say that they have found that they can do it. This certainly happened on numerous occasions when Yuri Geller was vandalising all that cutlery on TV shows, suddenly lots of people found that they were able to bend and twist their spoons. This phenomena, to a lesser degree, is evident in some people who are reluctant to shake hands, as they seem to either give out or receive a sudden jolt. It has been demonstrated that walking over a nylon carpet and perhaps wearing a nylon shirt allows the body to build up a powerful static electrical charge that eventually 'earths' perhaps in the aforesaid handshake or even touching the kitchen sink, if it is metal. The sink and the copper piping have already been earthed by the plumber, using earthing wire, to alleviate the substantial build-up of static electricity caused by flowing water through the piping. It may be possible, that some of the occasional break-up of our TV picture may be caused by the viewer himself rather than the atmospherics that are usually attributed to the fault.

Another factor displayed in TV shows dealing with the oddities of life has sometimes been portrayed where metal objects attach themselves to the body as though it was a powerful magnet, plates, knives, forks and spoons, even a heavy electrical iron.

There does not need to be anything, within reason, that the human body cannot affect in some way, even itself, when we consider voodoo and other native activity caused by Shamans or Witch Doctors. In some indictable practices, if proven, where the Witch Doctor puts a curse of death on a person, the victims own body augmented by the powerful force of the human mind does the rest and the victim often dies.

We have dealt with the mysterious N.D.E. or near death experiences, but there are people who claim that they can leave their body by their own volition, practically at will and travel about in an astral body, which can then detach itself from the physical body. How it utilises this ability is up to the person with this power. If, in normal body form, the person was a 'voyeur', it would be delighted to be able to travel 'in and out of the ladies chamber', but it would be rather disconcerting to those who value their privacy to have such a person around. Science had devoted some time to the analysis of this phenomena, but found little significance in the result. It is more probable, that only in bona fide N.D.E.s or in final termination, can the spirit leave the body. N.D.E.s obviously happens under different circumstances with no control over it, but what of the person claiming to be able to have full control over it? Does he sit thinking! I'm so bored I think I'll float off and see what old 'so and so' is up to".

One thing is certain, if such a person offered their services to the security organisations, they could name their price with regard to their salary.

Humans are certainly a strange breed when we witness the looting, pillaging and attacking the police and their vehicles, destroying historical monuments and so forth at the slightest excuse, we realise how thin the veneer of civilisation is, in some people. Fortunately they are in the minority, yet others plan trips to Mars.

In dealing with the many facets of the human mental makeup, there used to be a term 'religious mania', applied to some zealous religious people, who even cause harm to themselves by self-flagellation for example, but this moves into the realm of sexual perversions, such as masochism, but in the main, such people who morbidly dwell on the suffering Jesus went through, motivates them to cause pain to themselves.

The subject of 'stigmata' may be a close relation of this phenomena but not being a case of self-harm, but rather harm caused by the hidden powers of the human psyche.

Some cases of this phenomena, have proven to be fakery, although what motivates such people to perpetrate it, as a subject for the psychiatrists. Some people (who may fit into the category of masochism) have been known to pierce their own flesh, their hands, side and feet, to duplicate the wounds of Christ. The Catholic Church does not wholly embrace the subject of stigmata, and indeed rejects the notion of possession and leans toward the causes as mental aberration. One of the most high profile cases or stigmata was apparent on the body of a priest named Padre Pio of Italy. He lived from 1887 to 1968. He visibly bled from his palms and other areas, again replicating the wounds of Christ.

However, far from being revered by the papal hierarchy as almost a 'saint in waiting', he was viewed with suspicion. This would not help the situation when people where drifting away from the church, where the 'post Darwin' era had set in and the lukewarm Christians, in some cases, where moving toward the teachings of the 'New Messiah', Charles Darwin.

In the case of Padre Pio, where he could have been held up as an example of god's workings, they (in modern parlance) had their chance and blew it, instead, a papal investigative body was commissioned.

As a result of the enquiry, Padre Pio, the priest, was not allowed to hear confessions or deliver sermons during mass, but the church did not count on the Padre's popularity among the congregation. The masses did not take kindly to the way the church treated him. A first class example of public pressure the church obviously realised this is not the way to win worshippers and influence them.

However, the pressure paid off and the church, probably reluctantly, had him partly reinstated. He was allowed to say just one mass a day and take confessions on a limited basis. His first customer probably, during the routine preamble said "Forgive me father for I have sinned, I confess to daubing a slogan on the church wall saying 'support your local Padre'".

In the (sadly) cynical and 'science orientated' world of today, we seem to have little time for a 'blind faith' attitude and prefer to question and probe into the mental issues attached to the subject of stigmata and of course the mental stability of the 'stigmatee', but as said, it is not one for the church to answer but the psychiatrists who have barely scratched the surface, when laying bare the idiosyncrasies of the human entity. However, great work has been done and many positive advances have been made, that have led to successful treatment of mental issues. However, it has to be said, that much tranquillising, subduing through medication still prevails in the place of cures in some cases.

With regard to occurrences, that sometimes venture into the spiritual or paranormal (if there is a difference), almost everyone can recall an incidence in their childhood, that puzzled them so much at the time, yet the passage of time has not enabled them to get to the bottom of it, and certainly the memory remains.

I have mentioned my experience regarding my lost school lunch money, but going back further to my infant school days, shortly before progressing to the next grade. Each morning, when we passed along a corridor to our respective classes, we had to pass a large and obviously heavy statue of Christ. It stood on a large square block or plinth that was not separate from, but was part of the sculpture, it was place by a window that, along with others, one could look down on the school playground below. One day just as the bell to return to class was sounding, I looked up to the window above and the figure of Christ was in appearance looking down into the school yard, arms slightly outstretched (as it was formed), I saw the eyes, the long hair, beard and moustache but mostly notably the 'Sacred Heart' emblem (often seen in religious icons) that was sculptured into the front of the statue.

It took less than a minute to get back into the corridor, I made a point of heading for the statue, and it was still in its usual position, looking inward into the corridor. The teachers had not yet emerged from the restroom and we were always seated before the teacher came in. obviously, people will say, that the teachers turned the heavy statue to look down upon us during play, but it was a heavy unit and our teachers were all rather slight in build, in any case I could not imagine them hurrying to the statue to turn it back again, (it being rather heavy) then scampering back to the restroom to finish their tea. Nevertheless, the possibility exists (and again) I would not have hired a lawyer over the issue, even if I was old enough. It goes down into ones memory as something that stays.

It is no bad thing to have a healthy cynicism on such occurrences, but those who reject all aspects of the paranormal, should remember the words of Shakespeare "There are more things in Heaven and Earth than are dreamt of in your philosophy Horatio".

CHAPTER III

SUNK BUT NOT FORGOTTEN

One can imagine Zeus and the hierarchy of gods, in the cloudy fleecy domain, shaking with mirth, at Plato's frustration, as he yelled down to Earth, with nobody listening (or able to listen) to his protests.

"For goodness sake, check your history and get your facts right, I never said Santorini (Thera) was Atlantis, I said it was beyond the pillars of Hercules and Hercules is right here to confirm it, not within them. The Mediterranean is little more than an inland harbour. Don't you think I can add? I said 9000 BC not 1400 BC. It was in the true ocean, you dolts".

Zeus rose and placed a hand on Plato's shoulder and said "Calm yourself Plato, the truth will out". he offered Plato a goblet of nectar.

To return to reality, there is no doubt that if the books that have been written regarding the mutual lost continent of Atlantis, where laid like stepping stones, they would probably stretch from Plato's birthplace to the middle of the Atlantic and back again.

During the time of Plato (360 BC) the major volcanic explosion of Santorini/Thera had occurred some, one thousand plus years beforehand. The ancient Egyptian had enormous history behind them and related this to visiting Greek travellers, which is how The real story of Atlantis was first revealed. To a Greek traveller called Solon. 9000 BC would not seem so remote to the Egyptians when their history seems to have stretched back many thousands of years into the past. The Egyptian priests, often enlightened visiting Greek scholars of many things, and mentioned that previous eras of mankind had experienced very severe and destructive earthly conflagrations, stating "There have been and will be more such catastrophes, where humankind have to begin again as children". This was related to the Greek traveller Solon and this is how Plato became aware of the story received by his predecessors.

Modern 'Atlantologists' have suggested many and varied places where Atlantis could have existed, in this regard, it could be compared to the equally widespread suggestions regarding the once existing 'Camelot' or King Arthurs Court, that encompass the length and breadth of Britain from North to South in all the claims.

However, Plato was an educated and quite learned man and was not sloppy when defining dates and locations regarding areas that he wrote about in his works 'Critias' and 'Timaeus'. He was quite specific in his clearly stated location of the lost continent of Atlantis. However, in spite of this, there are those who will choose their own particular locations for it, in order to fit in with their own theories and research. Plato was well aware of his equally learned predecessors regarding the time in which they lived, their writings, theories and so forth and was quite specific about dates, which must be a little disturbing to him in his spiritual form, when he is contradicted, but not able to answer.

This would be particularly irritating for him (if he were aware of it) when seeing his facts, figures and dates being manipulated in order to site the theories of others, as though Plato had been suffering from some kind of dementia and mixing up his dates and also the inference that he could not get his sums right.

We mentioned the most well known of Plato's writings, that is the Timaeus and Critias that contain his writings on Atlantis and the tragedy that befell it. Plato did in such writings, make it clear that the account of the Atlantis saga was not his own story and that it was recorded by Solon.

Solon was a 'law giver' of Ancient Greece, who travelled extensively and found himself in Egypt (some two hundred years before Plato's time) at around 560 BC.

Solon was in contact with the Hieratic College of Learning in Sais. He learned from the knowledgeable priests that the Egyptian archives where thousands of years old and in these records, it was related that there had been a lost continent 'beyond the pillars of Hercules that was submerged in a catastrophe in 9,560 BC. Of course 'BC' would have meant nothing to them, it is a modern day standpoint for our own calculations of the date.

We have said that this date was over nine thousand years before Plato's time, but it indicates the awareness of the 'ancientness' of Egyptian history. Within the story of the Atlantean catastrophe, a clear indication of the continent 'beyond' it, or west of it, could only be an awareness of the coast of America that was still to be discovered. Certain writings have suggested that really ancient voyagers, including the mapmakers that drew an accurate chart of every cove and inlet of the Antarctic Coast, now deeply covered in ice, arrived in North American lands also, and later the Nordic travellers from Scandinavia in pre-Columbian times.

Plato made it clear that the true ocean (as we have said) 'beyond the pillars of Hercules' was most assuredly the site of the Atlantean sea. He also made it clear that the area or geographical size of Atlantis was larger than Libya and Asia Minor put together.

Obviously all these factors prohibit any comparison with the relatively tiny island of Thera/Santorini. As for its population, Plato wrote of its army and navy comprising of one million two hundred and ten thousand men. This of course would indicate an island population of multimillions of people as the armed forces of any nation, only ever represent but a small portion of the entire population of any country. Plato himself admitted that many people would find it hard to believe that his narrative was true, but he was adamant that it was.

Plato mentions that the buildings in Atlantis where constructed of white, black and red coloured stones. Strangely, stones of these colours can be found in the islands of the Azores, suggested as being part of the oceanic remnants of Atlantis.

When suggesting the remains of Thera/Santorini as being the skeleton of Atlantis, there is a noticeable lack of red, white and black stones there. The island mass exploded in 1400 BC and left a large crater, with parts of the island remaining in a circular fashion. Of course, regarding the date of its demise as 1400 BC is our date, in Plato's time, as we have mentioned, it would be just over one thousand years before his era, but with regard to the disappearance of Atlantis, it would have occurred about nine thousand years before him.

Plato, in his account states, "In those times, the Atlantic was navigable from an island situated to the west of the straits of Gibraltar. When referring to the 'true ocean', this negates any reference to the Aegean Sea of the Mediterranean. When Plato refers to the 'ten kings of Atlantis in his story, there would certainly be enough room for ten 'kingdoms' in the area stated regarding its size, but certainly not in the small land mass of Santorini/Thera, which is said to be only some seventy five square miles in land area. Yet the claims still remain that it was the lost continent, but the contradictions are too obvious. The academician V.A. Obrutchev of the former USSR, was of the opinion, that the legend of Atlantis was not impossible to accept from a geological standpoint. In addition, a professor N. Ledney, a Moscow born physicist and mathematician, after his lengthy research also came to the conclusion that the fabled Atlantis is no myth. Yet another Soviet scientist, E. Katarina Hagemeister pointed out that since the waters of the Gulf Stream, which are relatively warm, reached the Northern Arctic Ocean between ten to twelve thousand years ago, causing the cessation of the prevailing Ice Age, this must indicate the sudden loss of a major land barrier that allowed the warmer waters to flow much further north. The lost landmass was concluded to be Atlantis.

Atlantis, it was said, was the reason the Ice Age prevailed, but was also the cause of its demise. A Swedish vessel called the 'Albatross', when taking soundings off the sea bed of the Equatorial Atlantis, discovered traces of fresh water plants at a depth of over two miles down. The leader of the expedition, a certain Professor Hans Peterson could only assume that the area was once at sea level.

STRANGE REALITIES

Science is aware that there was a sudden warming of surface ocean waters in the Atlantic Ocean that took place around ten thousand years ago. These assumptions are based on the studies of foraminifera, tiny sea creatures with a shell. There are two different types that live in either warm water or cold and their distribution and their preferred locations suddenly changing at the above time supported their conclusions regarding the above estimated date.

The significant dates of ten to twelve thousand years ago crop up in many different areas of research. Some significant results have been obtained, using the radio carbon dating of various materials. A cedar forest grew at one time, on the 'Greater Bermuda', which is now under water. A very large landmass in the middle of an ocean would cause great water displacement and inundations. Scientists working for the Lamont Geological Observatory in the US and after their various studies, the conclusion seemed inescapable, that some catastrophic weather and climatic changes occurred in the Atlantic Ocean, close to the time that is frequently cited as the point when the mythical island disappeared.

The period of around ten thousand to twelve thousand years ago witnessed some quite intensive ocean floor movements. Waterfalls generally, are considered
to have formed when a fast flowing river, over millions of years, may flow over a riverbed where the harder sediments start to encounter less hardened material, therefore, the softer material will then start to wash away to the sea by the force of the flowing water and eventually, over long periods of time, will produce a higher and lower level of the water flow, and then it becomes self generating, faster flow cascading down into the lower level increased the erosive factors even more. Eventually the waterfalls iare up and running, but some waterfalls are so high that one is forced to consider whether other earthly forces have been involved to push up the land as in the tectonic force heaving up the eastern side of the Pacific i.e. the Peruvian Andes.

The age of the Niagara Gorge from the mouth of the river to the present water fall is some twelve thousand years and may have been rising for a couple of thousand years and it is notable that the rise of the cordillera to some nineteen thousand feet took place about ten hundred years ago. Other quite turbulent activity affecting the Pacific and the equally powerful forces of plate tectonics where continents meet and push vigorously together sometimes causing undersea tremors and even huge tsunamis, when one land mass gives way and slips beneath the other. It is estimated, that many millions of years should have been necessary to produce the higher waterfalls, such as Niagara (USA/Canada) and Victoria Falls in Africa. Other factors tend to support the theory that Atlantis did exist, lying between the continents of the USA and Africa, then it would make sense, that it would affect the culture, artifacts, constructions, tools of the same design and material and also similarities in language.

The Basques have a legend of a cataclysm in which 'fire and water were at war'. In addition, the Basque peoples are said to speak a tongue that has an inexplicable affinity with the American Indian dialects. A Basque missionary preached to the Indians in Petén, Guatemala in his native tongue, and was understood. Where it not for the fact that so many pages of written history of the world have been ripped out in constant and purposeful destruction of scrolls, parchments and philosophical works, we may already have the answers to many mysteries and legends (including Atlantis).

Geological and undersea expeditions of the earliest times would be very inconclusive today, given the continuous turmoil and upheaval under the Atlantic Ocean that has occurred and indeed, has prevailed over the Millennia. The sea floor is very turbulent with land sinking as well as rising that has prevailed since the alleged loss of the huge landmass said to have been the lost continent of Atlantis.

It has to be said, that the only convincing written account of the disaster, is that of Plato. The rest of the references are largely gathered from the myths, legends and the ancestral tales of the natives. A study of the few remaining Maya documents that survived the destructive religious zeal of the Conquistadores, show various symbols, diagrams and hieroglyphics that were discovered, which were depicted by the ancient artists, they tended to corroborate the natives' stories. To refer again to the legend of the arrival of the Moon, eventually, as traumatic as it was, over the Millennia it would gradually be taken for granted. Much like the astronomers when they discover a new planet. Lengthy periods of excited discussion and interest, then logged into recorded history and no longer discussed.

The Romans where in awe of the ancient Greeks and their culture but this reverence was not returned. The Roman poet Ovid was interested in the account, written by Plato regarding the destruction of the great island civilisation and part of his verses in this regard, read "Soon there was no telling the land from the sea, under the water, the sea nymphs where staring in amazement at houses, towns and cities and submerged woodlands. Nearly all men perished by drowning and those who escaped the water having no food died of hunger".

The last paragraph is interesting in that it implies people, still alive on the landmass or some kind of Desert Island, but a barren landscape affording them no hope of escape and nothing growing there.

In Egypt a three thousand year old document or twelfth dynasty, papyrus that is preserved at the Leningrad Hermitage mentions 'the island of the serpent' (thought to be referring to Atlantis) and contains the following passage, "After you leave my island, you will not find it again, as this place will vanish under the sea waves". Naturally, news of the catastrophe would soon reach the continents either side of the lost landmass and no doubt some of the survivors. It is written, that the Atlanteans where skilled seafarers and many islanders who were at sea at the time of its destruction, would surely have sailed east or west to survive.

Another part of the aforementioned Papyrus states, "When I saw the mountain of corpses I almost died of grief". The Maya must have been aware of the catastrophe, as part of a Mayan codex states "In one day all perished, even the mountains disappeared under the water".

Further evidence of the above type exists. The Chilam Balam of Yucatan asserts that 'the motherland' of the Maya (their origins) was swallowed up by the sea with fiery eruptions and earthquakes in a distant epoch.

These strange and enigmatic people, where highly advanced for their time, almost on a par with ancient Egyptians and it is suggested that both peoples originated in Atlantis.

The book 'Atlantis' by Andrew Tomas, says that a white Indian Tribe called the 'Paria' used to live in Venezuela, named their village 'Atlan'. They spoke of a calamity that destroyed their homeland that was a 'large island in the ocean'. All these accounts cannot be imaginative tales as they are all so similar and corroborative and certainly have no bearing on the destruction of Therea/Santorini, yet the supporters of it cling to the their preferred version at all costs.

Professor I A Efremov of the Soviet Union states, "Mythology and folklore can be used to some extent, in filling many gaps in world history". The legends of these land areas indicate that beings of great wisdom and learning arrived from a central Atlantic source. The word 'Aztlán' has an obvious resemblance to Atlantis and the Aztecs revered Quetzalcoatl the culture bearer who came from
the east. The Incas choice was Viracocha who also arrived 'from the land of dawn' (the east).

In the other direction, early Egyptian records speak of 'Thoth' who came from a 'western' land to plant civilisation and learning in the valley of the Nile.

Montezuma, the last King of the Aztecs told Cortez of the conquistadors, "Our fathers were not born here but came from a distant land called 'Aztlán' under the Ruler of a distant eastern empire (a king of Atlantis perhaps?). clearly when he said 'fathers', he was referring to distant predecessors.

With all these factors in mind, it seems to indicate that there was once an important empire situated centrally in the Atlantic, this conclusion seems inescapable.

However, one must remark, that for all their alleged wisdom, they seem to have had little knowledge or fear of volcanism and geological disturbances (if there were any), both on the surface and beneath the sea, particularly, as their assumed highly advanced island sat across the extremely volatile 'Atlantic Ridge'. Snaking along the length of the Atlantic Ocean from north to south (centrally).

However, ten thousand years ago, it may have been less active under the influence of the massive undersea forces that we now know as 'plate tectonics', but great inner disturbances of the Earth must have been felt when the first violence of the Earth occurred, the record of which may not even exist in their ancient myths and legends of twelve thousand years ago. This was two thousand years before the Atlantis catastrophe and that may have been the first tilt of the Earth to the twenty-six degree position, it turned twenty three and a half degrees but who was doing any writing or recording around 12,000 BC? However, we must remember, that many ancient Maya codices were purposely destroyed by the religious hierarchy of the conquistadors. The Earth would have shuddered, rumbled and felt the disturbances caused by the arrival of the Moon, which must have been felt also among the Atlantians as a forewarning, but ignored.

Those who 'put the case' for the actual existence and final destruction of Atlantis can quote many other similarities in culture, artifacts and buildings even similar games that were played by the natives in the doomed island that spread east and west. There are too many of these similarities to be put down to coincidence.

All the worldwide myths and legends that do refer to Atlantis indicate that the last day of the doomed island was a veritable doomsday and ended very quickly. Mountain sized waves, hurricanes and volcanic explosions, all contributed to its final demise.

As we have said, it is well known that the sea bottom of the Atlantic is a very volatile area. Land sinks and emerges from the sea floor in comparatively short periods of time. A smoking mountain arose from the depths of the Atlantic, near the Azores in 1957. Again, in the Azores some years later, an earthquake was experienced in St George Island causing fifteen thousand occupants to hurriedly flee from the island.

In the South Atlantic, the majority of the population of Tristan De Cunha were evacuated to England when a (thought to be extinct) volcano erupted. Although possibly a pale comparison, those who witnessed the eruption of the volcano that smothered Pompeii in the Bay of Naples and of course Krakatoa must have observed a similar scene to the Atlantis event. Of course, it is not only the Atlantic sea bottom that experiences these events, they occur to some degree all over the world.

It is said that the entire continent of France is sinking at the rate of thirty centimeters a century. Technicians aboard a 'western telegraph' ship, that was searching for a lost cable in the Atlantic in 1923, detected that the cable had been thrown up two and a half miles in only twenty five years by a rising ocean bed since it was laid.

It is claimed, although not accepted by some geologists, that south of the Azores there are to so-called 'seamounts' that are the parts of the dead body of the legendary Atlantis, we may have mentioned that Professor M Ewing of Columbia University explored the volatile mid Atlantic Ridge in 1949 and discovered 'beach sand' at depths of two miles and three and a half miles that should not exist on the seabed. Furthermore, some geologists say, that many undersea valleys in the Atlantic are nothing else than continuations of once existing surface rivers. There are numerous indicators that some places of the Atlantic sea bottom, must, in a past epoch, have been dry land.

Crantor (300 BC), stated that in Egypt, there were certain pillars in secret places, that told the entire history of Atlantis in hieroglyphics and that they were shown to visiting Greeks searching for knowledge of ancient Egypt. Such visitors may well have included Plato who preceded Crantor.

To reinforce the 'ancientness' of the Egyptian historical accounts and writings, two thousand five hundred years ago, Herodotus was shown three hundred and forty five statues in linear succession, of various Egyptian priests, going back into the past thousands of years before his time. Herodotus writes, "They seem to be quite certain of these dates, for they have always kept a careful record written regarding the passage of time".

Most people are aware of the loss of so many ancient writings, scrolls and parchments, that were purposely destroyed through ignorance or religious zeal. Andrew Tomas wrote, "It is known that the Serapeum and Brucheum in Alexandria contained over half a million priceless documents". Obviously, if we had access to all this data today, our view on ancient history, beliefs and legends would, change overnight and free us of all the guesswork and supposition that often goes with ancient legends.

There is a tradition, however, that shortly before the burning of Alexandria by the Romans, that some of the ancient manuscripts where saved. What a decision to have to make in a hurry, regarding which documents where the best to save. It would be interesting to know if an uncontrollable fire broke out in the British Library what books would one rush to preserve.

Cleopatra, the last of the Egyptian monarchs, may well have ordered this type of hurried action, in order to preserve at least some of their ancient history. Julius Caesar did not directly destroy the Brucheum, but it was caused by the fire that spread from his destruction of the Egyptian Fleet in the harbour of Alexandria, the fire spread to the city and engulfed the Great Repository.

When we return to the sea floor of the Atlantic Ocean, the sea floor beneath the Azores and further east towards the Canary Islands, life threatening volcanic activity never stops destroying and re-creating land in the turbulent activity below. With regard to the Atlantis story the sudden and catastrophic submergence of all the great edifices pillars, building and monuments fell, clearly, they would not descend like a lift in an office block, they would crumble and disintegrate onto their sides and thereafter, with regard to the aforementioned turbulent activity, ten thousand years of volcanic lava oozing from below, with other natural sediments, churned up oceanic currents etc., would surely have slowly but surely covered over all traces of any identical structures, the mid Atlantic ridge is very active and this would contribute greatly to the continuing changes on the Ocean floor.

Descending in a D.S.R.V. (deep-sea research vehicle) excitedly, expecting to see Atlantis ruins in their abundance would turn out to be very disappointing, and of course, this has occurred.

However, having said all that, the possibility that some edifices may still exist, some many have sunk, then been pushed up again in the aforementioned lowering and heaving up of the seabed.

In optimum weather conditions, the pilots of aircraft crossing the Atlantic, have observed certain symmetrical objects that have the appearance of being purposely constructed, yet often when trying to find them again fail to do so, they cannot guarantee that they are passing over the exact same spot, unless of course, they purposely logged and recorded them. However, of course, doing so may invoke some comments from the airline directors "You're not on an oceanic sightseeing tour; concentrate on the job in hand". Nevertheless, because of these types of sightings they came to the attention of the institute of the underwater technology.

A former Yale University Professor J Manson Valentine formed an expedition that resulted in the discovery of what may have been a temple, near the north end of the Andros Island, which is the largest island in the Bahamas. The conclusion goes, that if one discovers a temple, then some kind of town, city, or metropolis must accompany it.

Of course, cynics and rationalists will point out that nature's forces both on land and undersea, can cause interesting shapes and formations to be shaped by sea currents and so forth that can give rise to many incorrect assumptions. This is true of course, when we consider 'Monument Valley' in the US and the Giant Causeway in Northern Island, yet this only applies when viewed from afar. The underwater diving team in the J Manson Valentine Expedition obtained many close up views of those edifices.

However, there is one thing that nature's forces can never do, and that is to form a perfect square with ninety-degree corners, that is always going to be the work of humans.

Dr Valentine and his team discovered many geometrical and circular edifices, polygonal flat stones of various sizes and thicknesses under the sea for sixty miles from Bimini to Orange Cay.

Another expedition, this time led by the famous Jacques Cousteau and his team on the ship 'Calypso', discovered a huge grotto of undersea caves that contained stalactites and stalagmites. there was no question about the fact that such formations can only occur above the ground.

It was scientifically ascertained that the area was submerged twelve thousand years ago (the arrival of the Moon perhaps?) but an analysis of the stalagmites by a group of scientists in Miami, showed that a violent geological upheaval occurred in the Atlantic Basin around ten thousand years ago (Atlantis?). this date continually crops up throughout history when referring to the catastrophic events.

When we look back at the myths, stories and accounts that refer to Atlantis, they all focus back on the era of Solon rather than Plato, whose account came much later. Solon the Greek Historian, was given the full story by the Egyptian wise ones, who considered the Greeks as young, still in the learning mode and with little ancient history that was 'hoary with age', as Plato later recorded it.

It became clear to Solon, that the Egyptians had an extremely lengthy history. Long after Solon had passed away, Plato inherited the story. It had remained and had kept its details clear and unchanged. Today, after some ten thousand years, one would have expected that it would have been embellished beyond recognition with many additions and some omissions, but the survival of Plato's Critias and Timaeus in fragments ensured this did not happen.

Diogenes Laurtius wrote in 300 AD, that the ancient Egyptians had recorded three hundred and seventy three solar, and eight hundred and thirty two lunar eclipses. On the basis of the periodicity of eclipses, it can be estimated that this would cover a period of ten thousand years.

The story related to Solon about the loss of Atlantis was certainly not a myth or legend being clearly installed in the Egyptian records. Nevertheless, their credibility is somewhat stretched when learning that the Byzantine historian George Syncellus (AD 806), wrote of the 'chronicles' that the ancient Egyptians had kept for thirty six thousand five hundred and twenty five years.

Andrew Tomas, in his account of Atlantis in 1972 writes, that Proclus (AD 412-489) stated that Plato himself, visited Egypt and conversed at Sais with an Egyptian High Priest Pateneit at Heliopolis, therefore, any omissions or additions and doubts about Solon's version could be easily cleared up and put right. This of course indicates the accuracy of detail would be depicted in Plato's version.

As said, Thoth, the earliest of the Egyptian sages was said to have come from the Island that had existed 'in the western sea'. He and other wise ones may have foreseen the disaster to come, in which case, there would be no question of the validity of the loss of his former homeland, as it would have been given to the earliest Egyptian scribes and subsequently been passed down through the ages of the Egyptian long history.

Although we attribute a great knowledge and wisdom to the ancient Greeks, we must recognise that much of their knowledge would have been obtained from earlier sources. Nevertheless, they have secured their place in history.

Isaac Newton once said, "If I have seen further, it is by standing on the shoulders of giants". We have mentioned Proclus, he stated, "The Famous Atlantis no longer exists, but we can hardly doubt that it once did". Centuries before Proclus, the historian Strabo said, "It is possible that the story about the island of Atlantis is not fiction".

We mentioned that there were two possible conflagrations, the first, when we assume that the Moon could have arrived in Earth space, tilting the Earth from an almost vertical position to some twenty-six degrees with all the disastrous earthly upset that followed. Then the latter lurched back again to our twenty-three degree tilt of today, producing more earthly mayhem possibly causing the Biblical flood that Moses was happy to relate in writing Genesis. If the coming of the Moon had occurred a couple of thousand years earlier the story would be 'old hat' and the people would be well used to its presence, as we have said. Nevertheless, the story may once have existed in the earlier forms of writing and possibly destroyed along with many other stories that the ancients could not accept as true, but with regard to the seemingly unstable axis of the Moon, any deviation would cause earthly mayhem and great loss of life, but not all human life clearly, those who had survived (there are always survivors) who may have been on much higher ground in the sunlight areas, up the mountains with their flocks, would see the sun reeling and obviously 'moving' similarly those on high ground at night star gazing as they watched their flocks, would observe the stars appearing to slip away of 'fall into the sea' or 'the sky fell down'.

Martinus Martini, a 17th century Jesuit, was a missionary in China. In his *History of China* after studying her oldest records, stated, "These stories speak of a time when the sky suddenly fell northwards; the Sun and the planets changed their courses after the Earth had been shaken".

This shows, that accounts from all over the world, have produced their own written legends from the ancient tales passed down from previous generations. Atlantis and the mid Atlantic Ridge below it may have been severely rent asunder allowing Magma from beneath the Earth to slowly weaken its foundations eventually resulting in its destruction and collapse.

There is a bushman's tale from Africa, related by Andrew Tomas in his book *Atlantis* that mentions a vast landmass, which had existed 'west of Africa', that was later submerged. It is quite significant that there are tales and legends regarding this major event that would emerge from both sides of the Atlantic, particularly if the respective cultures displayed similar roots and cultural ties.

Regarding the conflagration and subsequently loss of the island, a Maya codex stated, "In one day, all perished, even the mountains disappeared under the water". The Mayan Moon Goddess was the patroness of 'death' (significant, regarding all we have related). The sacred book of the Guatemala Maya that is, the Popol Vuh says, "The Earth shook the trees where shaking and the houses crumbling".

It would seem, that the earthly violence that prevailed through the centuries, did not only have its affects on the east and west sides of the Atlantic i.e. South America and Africa but as far north as the land of the Eskimos and the Chinese, the legend states that "The Earth tilted violently before a great flood came".

Obviously, it must have been a very rapid event for legends to be stating that the Earth tilted noticeably and observations of the sun and stars moving in the heavens. Some accounts may seem very difficult to accept but the fact remains that there are too many of them to be assumed that some important person must have had a believable nightmare and related it, like Hiawatha warning of his 'vision' regarding the coming of the white men. The core event of the tilting of the Earth remains firmly in place.

To mention Andrew Tomas again, he says, "Two star maps, painted on the ceiling of the Tomb of Senmouth, who was Queen Hatshepsut's architect, present a riddle in that the cardinal points (north, south, east and west) are correctly placed on one of these astronomical charts but on the other, they are reversed denoting an earthly tilt. In fact, the Harris Papyrus mentioned that the Earth had 'turned over' in a past cosmic cataclysm.

There are other papyruses that further support this theory. They state the Earth turned completely upside down. They are the Hermitage Papyrus of Leningrad and the Ipuwer Papyrus that allude to this major event. We have mentioned in other works regarding the woolly mammoths that were suddenly and violently transported to the far north and frozen solid some were found still in the standing position, which highlights just how rapid the event was.

The theory that this event was due to the crust of the Earth sliding over the semi-molten magma under the more solid surface, could not possibly happen that fast, especially when we consider the creeping slow continental drift theory.

A sudden and rapid change in the Earth's axial position is the only plausible answer. The event would cause all living creatures to experience rapidly different seasons appearing then passing by as the tilt took place. The following story seems to bear this out.

The Indians, living in the lower regions of the Mackenzie River in Northern Canada, maintain that during the deluge an unbearable heat wave came suddenly, the heat was followed by a severe frost, only a rapidly tilting Earth could account for this event.

However, the tilt would appear to be more of a rocking event, followed by a northern tilt and settling at that angle. The latitude of the Indians being northern, then in order to produce the said heat would be the affect of them being rapidly tilted toward an equatorial latitude, then back again to the north. Clearly, the survivors would have been so traumatised by the event; they would feel compelled to record it all for further generations.

If a pyramid culture did exist on the mythical lost continent then this would explain it as an attempt at revival when we see it displayed in South America, the Nile Delta, and its route south.

I referred earlier to my book *When the Moon Came*. The Preface referred to a Government astronomer and director of the Adelaide Observatory George F Dodwell. His twenty six year studies and investigation of the movements of the Earth's axis, seemed to indicate a sudden change in the angle of the Earth's axis from a former near vertical position, to a tilt of twenty six and a half degrees, then a gradual recovery to a position of what we know today, which is twenty three and a half degrees.

Formerly there would have been very little seasonal effects on Earth. As we know, as well as the equatorial latitude, there is another latitude above it, we call The Tropic of Cancer and another below it called The Tropic of Capricorn. When the Earth travels around the Sun, because of its tilt it presents a gradual movement of the sun's strength as it swept north and south of the equator giving us our seasons.

However, as the Moon approached the Earth it wrenched the Earth into its new substantial twenty-six and a half degrees position. Immediate season effect would have been experienced perhaps accounting the statements in ancient writings of "The stars slipping into the sea" and the sudden movements of the Sun etc. Initially there would have been a great havoc on Earth with much destruction, Tsunamis and loss of life. No wonder the Mayan Moon goddess signified death. It is little wonder that Moon worship cults did arise. Those that survived where moved to placate the Moon by any means possible in their gratitude for their own survival. I mentioned in *When the Moon Came*, that the Aleutian Islanders stoned people to death for offending the Moon, but also asked, "How would they manage to offend it?"

However, the Moon had not finished offending the Earth. We could use the analogy of a poor old gentleman riddled with arthritis, continually shifting about trying to find the least painful position to sit. The Moon groaned and shuddered, due to the earthly forces over the centuries, until eventually, it shifted itself back to a more favourable position. Ah.... That is much better this new twenty-three and half-degree position will do very nicely.

But now the Earth had to endure its second fearful disruptive conflagration and deaths due to the selfish old Moon wanting to make itself more comfortable.

Now the ancient symbols, glyphs, and people depicted worshipping an orb (interpreted as either Sun worship or even UFO today) makes sense. It was so that primitive peoples could record their trauma. Eventually such depictions developed, due to the flowering of the intellect and of artistic ability. The learned ones became the scribes, recorders and historians of their time, with information that they hoped would tell the true story of what they had gone through on Earth.

Although they used the strongest material for their written works, there were no photocopy machines to retain copies of their work and so the negative actions of lesser humans undid all their hard work through sheer destruction.

We mourn the loss of such documents that could have told us so much about the dark part of our world history. But all was not lost, verbal accounts, passed down through the generations in snippets here and there and this time the Moon's restless shifting about was revealed through the various stories that exist here and even though they are all we have, it is said historians must pay more respect to these ancient accounts and traditions. We must state, however, that there is a strange paradox between the alleged occurrence on the Earth's surface and all the convincing verbal and written data, in comparison to the evidence on the seabed, but then we must consider the thousands of years of seabed turbulent activity over the millennia.

The natural development of the human brain and its understandable inclination to explain things in a logical and orderly manner, resulted in the aforementioned engravings, glyphs and symbols, that soon developed into hieroglyphics strung together which is clearly a form of writing and can be read by Egyptologists for example, who can interpret the meaning of the glyphs, but an ancient form of writing must have existed even before the Egyptian culture flourished, if only we could read all the old manuscripts, lost in destructive wars, fires, and purposeful destruction, that had found themselves indexed by their thousands (probably millions) into the ancient repositories.

The history of the human is full of strange paradoxes. The high intelligence of the human on one side, that was responsible for all those intellectual accounts and the fact that ignorance and fear of the unknown also exists, that caused their destruction, such acts sully the more positive and advanced facets of the human brain, but they have always existed.

This fear of the unknown still prevails, why else would our military attempt to eliminate a technology that is so far advanced of our own by trying to destroy it? If it was not so, we may well be conversing with and learning from a higher civilisation.

But we must conclude by saying that although an abundance of circumstantial evidence exists, for the alleged disappearance of the lost continent of Atlantis, and in spite of the convincing account by Plato, and the fact that he and his predecessor Solon did exist, who both provided such a detailed story, nothing has changed.

In addition, so far, all that, plus the substantial amount of backup in the aforesaid legends, when it comes down to producing actual proof of the dramatic loss of the mythical island .... We are sunk.

CHAPTER IV

I CLIMBED ONTO NOAH'S ARK

The story of a worldwide deluge, rather than a major flood occurring in the Middle East, is given credence by the fact that flood legends exist all over the world in the ancient records of most countries. The core ingredients being the hero who saves his family and the righteous ones (and animals) to repopulate the world later.

The most enduring one is the Biblical account in Genesis. To believe the story for Noah and his ark implies a belief in the entire Genesis writings where of course, the creation event of the universe, the world, Adam and Eve and all worldly creatures was tidied up in a week.

Nevertheless, the Biblical story of Noah's life does prevail. The onset of search teams, to scour the mountains of Ararat began after an aircraft flying over the area photographed an object that resembled the shape of a large boat. Further excitement was aroused when the dimensions came fairly close to those mentioned in Genesis, that were given to Noah in terms of the Biblical cubit.

The author Rene Noorbergen, states that some eighty thousand books pertaining to the universal deluge have been written in many languages. With regard to Genesis, he devoted many years of research. He became acquainted with a group that was setting out to explore Mount Ararat in Eastern Turkey to search for remnants of the legendary Ark of Noah. He returned to the United States from a second ark expedition in the late sixties.

Clearly, Rene Noorbergen, as indeed, were many academic and learned people, moved to find proof among them. Professor Arthur J Brandenburger, specialist in photogrammetry of Ohio State University, where quite convinced (or perhaps wanted to be convinced) of the validity of the worldwide deluge, as the ancient memory of it has endured for at least five thousand years.

Rene Noorbergen relates, "In the preparation for the 1970 probe of Mount Ararat, a million piece mailing programme had been organised for the search foundation by a Colonel Pak, head of The Freedom and Cultural Foundation of Korea".

After a few weeks, some six hundred thousand pieces of mail where dropped through American mailboxes as promotional literature. Our present name for this is 'junk mail' and one supposes many people discarded it as such. Nothing much has changed in the last fifty years as half of my mail is disposed of under this category. Nevertheless, a most positive result was achieved. At the headquarters of the Foundation, a real estate broker, in

Easton, Maryland, stated that an old friend of hers, a certain George Hagopian, an aged Armenian living in the US, used to live right at the foot of the mountain and thought perhaps the Foundation would be interested in talking to him.

Enter, the man who (as a young boy) claimed to have climbed onto the petrified hulk of the ark, now turned to stone, George Hagopian.

At the time of his meeting with the members of the proposed ark expedition, George was over eighty, but he was quite lucid and articulate when relating his story. Also, it was quite apparent that George's memory of the event was quite clear with regard to all the detail he provided for the research team, who could not believe their luck in finding such a witness. Such is the power of advertising, with regard to the many items of promotional mail they sent out.

George's account to the team was recorded from start to finish and was not simply accepted as heard, it was subjected to the so-called 'psychological stress evaluation' (P.S.E. lie detector process) and it passed.

The expeditions that had set out previously, were not deterred by the many comments that it was a lost cause, and the legend, if it really happened, could not possibly produce remnants of a ship, that may have been washed up there after such an amount of time. Nevertheless, the scientific members where of the opinion that the weather conditions, together with the purified air, where not conductive to wood rotting very quickly and petrification could occur over a long time period. The aforesaid event that started all the interest and search teams being formulated etc., was a Turkish Air Force pilot flying over Ararat.

It was said, that a US Air Force Base nearby, once determining the map reference of the boat shaped configuration, scheduled flights, partly through navigational exercises and partly through giving those who where religiously oriented, a chance to see it, which they may never get again, and if it turned out to be true they could 'dine out' on the story ever after.

One thing is for certain, George Hagopian believed it why wouldn't he? He had climbed onto it. It was George Hagopean's uncle who took young 'Georgy' as he called him, up the mountain from the lower area where he lived. His uncle through his experience and knowledge of the seasons knew the best time to try and reach the ancient hulk.

George began by stating that when he was a young boy, he had his uncle, when herding their quite large flock of sheep, would climb the mountain and when it got dark; they had many problems warding off the many incursions of wolves and bears and where glad of their dogs and their protective ability to run around barking and keeping the more adventurous predators from snatching a young lamb.

George's grandfather was the Minister of the Armenian Orthodox Church, in Van and often told stories to George, especially those regarding the 'Holy Mountain', which George listened to enthralled.

George's uncle, not only believed in the actual existence of the ark, he had seen it close up himself. George said that he was about ten years old when (probably due to George's continual questions) his uncle finally agreed to take him up to see the 'holy ark'.

His uncle had told him that, 'Massis' is the Holy Mountain. Soon, they packed up their equipment and secured it to the donkey and began their trek up the mountain. George said that it took them around eight days from the time they left Van, to finally reach the point where his uncle had told him was the final resting place where the Holy Ship had come aground.

George's uncle, through experience, knew that weather patterns that occur around the mountains and told George, that he had purposely chosen this particular time to make the trip because it was what the elders called 'a smooth year', that is, a year that occurs from time to time when there is little snow, which happens very rarely.

When they finally reached their destination, George was a little tired through constantly having to heave and guide the donkey back on track, as it always wanted to go another way. He said to his uncle "It is so dark and misty, did the ark really come to rest all the way up here?" His uncle replied, "Yes, this is the Holy Ark, the big ship is right in front of you Georgy".

George was aware of a great stone mass that lay in front of him, that he thought was a wall. He asked, "Is this really the ship uncle? This is not wood it is stone". And he touched the great mass in front of him as if to verify his opinion. His uncle chuckled and said, "It's the ship alright Georgy, I'll prove it to you, I will help you to climb onto it, come and help me".

George explained that he joined his uncle in selecting out stones of a more rectangular type that they could position at the base of the mass to build steps to help him reach the top of what he had earlier perceived as a 'wall'. George told the group that his uncle was a big and powerful man and was well over six foot tall. After some time, with George's help, they had piled the stones in such a manner that George could easily ascend part of the way up the 'wall.

At that point, George's uncle grabbed his arm and said, "Come here George, you're going to go on top of the Holy Ark". His uncle lifted him up onto his broad shoulders and they began to step up higher and higher on the stones until they reached the stage where they could go no further. At that point, his uncle grabbed George's feet and began to push him higher up the 'wall'. His uncle shouted out to George "Reach for the top Georgy", and told him to feel for the edge and when he found it to pull himself up.

George then had become quite excited about what he was about to see and related that he stood up as straight as he could and found that he could look over the top of what he now believed was the Holy Ship.

George said, "It was long alright, but not all of it was visible. Looking back now, I m sure that the part I saw must have been at least a hundred feet long and very wide. I would estimate the height of it at one side as being about forty feet high".

George's uncle called up to him from below and said, "Take a look inside Georgy, look for the holes, look for the big one and tell me what you see". George looked at the recorder and continued, "I was shivering at that point, it must have been due to excitement, as I had not felt the cold up to that point, but I was afraid now, I glanced around me, yes, there was a hole, big and gaping. This must be the hole uncle had told me to look for. It all looked so mysterious and I called out to my uncle that I was scared".

"I felt nervous and shouted down to my uncle, yes, there is a large hole, uncle I'm scared, I see a large black hole on top, but don't make me go in there please". My uncle replied, "Don't be scared Georgy, there is no one in the Ark. It's been empty for a long time". George then said, "I peeked into the blackness of the hole but I saw nothing, then I knelt down and kissed the Holy Ark".

At this point, one might be wondering how there could be a hole, as it surely should be full up with snow all the way to the top, however, some drawings of the Ark have been made by studying the various accounts that the sides of the Ark tapered up as they rose and that the top had a series of holes running along its length. On top of them was a 'roof like' structure, that would cause the rain and flood water to cascade away from the holes, but George never mentioned this.

Before George continued, one of the group asked him, "Did you see anything else while you were up there? any other distinguishing marks that we might use for identification, if we ever manage to locate the object?" George then replied "Oh yes many things. I noticed that there was a lot of moss and that this greenish growth seemed to cover most of the structure. When we were there, the top of the Ark was covered with a thin coat of freshly fallen snow, but when I began to brush some it away, the green moss I told you about, covered all of the top".

George then related how he "Got down on his knees and managed to wrench a piece of it off. It was then that I realised that this big structure, that I thought was made of stone was actually constructed of wood. I knew this was so because

I could plainly make out the grain of the wood, I would see the run of the grain right there below me".

George then related how his uncle took hold of his gun and shot a bullet into the side of the Ark, but that the bullet simply bounced off the structure, "The whole Ark", he said, "Had turned into rock".

Then another member of the group said, "Did you see anything more on the roof, other than the large hole you mentioned?" George answered, "Yes, I remember that there were a number of small holes that ran toward the rear of the structure, but I don't remember counting them but there were quite a few of them, they were in the middle of the vessel's roof and there where small intervals between them".

"When I was talking about them later, with my uncle, I asked him what he thought they were for and he told me they were for air. He said, a long time ago, there use to be many animals and people in the Ark and that there was one special hole, where Noah let the dove fly out". George then asked his uncle, "But where did they all go?", his uncle just said, "They just left Georgy, they're gone, the Holy Ship is completely empty now". George then described how his uncle drew a long hunting knife from his belt and chipped a large piece off the side of the Ark. "I suppose it must have been moss. He couldn't cut into petrified wood, but maybe he hoped that he could".

George continued, "I felt that I wanted to get down again off the top of the Ark, and I shouted down to my uncle that I was getting scared and that I now wanted to get off. I made to get down and my uncle once again, took a firm grip of my ankles and soon we started on our way back down the mountain".

"I couldn't wait to meet up with my grandfather again, so as soon as I had rested up, I hurried over to see him. Grandfather, I said, excitedly, "I have been to see the Holy Ark". George, at this point recalls getting an emotional hug from his grandfather.

This is certainly an interesting story and George Hagopain did not seem to be the kind of person that would lie, but was honest and open, and of course, we must remember the tape passed the 'lie detector test'. Therefore, he clearly believed in his own mind that it was true. "But this is just it", the sceptics would say, it could have been 'just in his own mind', after all the P.S.E. test will register favourably if you believe what you're saying is true".

George had admitted, that he had often spoken with his uncle and grandfather about it and could have experienced vivid dreams about it, mentally inserting bits here and there, regarding what he imagined it would be like. When one dreams, one (mostly) believes it is a scene really happening. I said mostly, because I can recall as a boy of around ten years old (the same age George was) having a vivid dream that made no sense but the difference was I knew I was dreaming. It involved a group of people grey and unrecognisable, seated around a semi-circular table and I was standing as if I was on some sort of trial. I suppose I must have felt threatened because I can clearly recall saying to the group "You can't do anything to me, this is just a dream and I know I will wake up soon".

I never experienced anything like that again but it shows the many facets of the mind. In the case of George, if he had dreamt it, then this would have come out in general conversation such as "What are you talking about Georgy, you've never been up there". There were other points we could raise but not regarding the validity of the story.

We could mention, that George's uncle often spoke with reverence about the 'Holy Mountain' and the 'Holy Ark', yet this did not seem to bother him when he shot a bullet at the Ark. Added to this is the obvious irresponsibility of risking a ricochet that could have injured or even killed either of them.

Also, as the uncle knew there was a large hole on top of the Ark, and that it was misty, it was obviously dangerous to George who could have fallen into it. If the uncle was as big and powerful as George had said he was, it would have made more sense if the uncle climbed up first, then pulled George up after him and made sure he was safe regarding the holes.

Finally, if the uncle knew so much about the Ark, that seemed to imply that he himself had visited it on his own and climbed onto it, then why did he not mention it?

Nevertheless, this was an intriguing story and ought to have been widely published with camera crews and producers struggling to interview George with major headlines appearing all over the world. It was fifty years ago when this interview occurred and the author who was present at the recorded interview with George, did put it all down to his book *Secrets of the Lost Races*. One hopes for his sake, that it was not a hoax.

Some expeditions in attempts to find the elusive Ark must have been made after this story, but George did not say he told anyone else. Certainly, the uncle could have, in his day, made a very good financial living as a tour guide. However, in the early seventies the Cold War was still at its peak and some of the cited locations that could be the Ark, or at least remnants of it, where not all reachable from the Turkish side of the region, therefore investigating groups had to be very careful not to tread on other peoples territory (or toes). Furthermore, we recognise of course the fact that 'Atheism' of the communists regime and Christianity are at opposite ends of the spectrum, so it was not just a question of packing up and going.

Also, the USSR at the time would not have been too excited about confirming the reality of a Genesis story. But we would also have to look behind the story of Noah, the Ark and the flood. We would need to believe in a divine creative God who must have made mistakes in his creation of the human stock, and had to wipe them out except for a few and start again.

Science, in the main, views most, if not all of the Genesis story. However, meticulously recorded in the Old Testament as little more than unscientific mysticism.

But to return to the story of George Hagopian, the team continued to question him, in the hope of obtaining any more snippets of information, however small, that may be useful to them later, even if they may have seemed insignificant to George and not worth mentioning. In this, they carried on talking to George for another few hours.

Towards the end of the interview with George, they asked him if he ever got the chance to see the Ark again. "Yes", replied George, "I did see the Ark again, I think it was in 1904, we were on the mountain a second time, looking for 'Holy Flowers', I went back to the Ark and it still looked the same, nothing had changed. I didn't climb on top of it this time but stayed at the side and got a really good look at it. It was resting on a steep ledge of bluish green rock which was very wide".

George paused as though recollecting his thoughts. "Something else I noticed, was that I didn't see any nails at all, it seemed as though the entire ship was made out of one piece of petrified wood. But I could definitely see the grain of the wood".

George was asked, "What about any other noticeable features, I mean, did you see any windows, portholes or doors? Anything of that nature?". After a few seconds George replied "Oh no, there were no windows in the ship, I'm certain of that, there was definitely no door on the side of the ship that I could see, and no opening of any kind, but there may have been such on the side that I could not see, that side was practically inaccessible, I could only see my side and also part of the bow".

Another question was fired at George, "What was the overall shape of the vessel? Was it perfectly straight, rectangular or what?". There was a slight distraction at that point and they all waited until things settled down. George replied, "The roof was flat, with the exception of that narrow raised section running along the top with all those holes in it. The sides where slanting upwards towards the top, and the front of the ship was flat too".

We could mention a couple of points regarding the shape of 'the bow', one would have thought that one of the expedition team would have asked George, "How do you know whether you where looking at the bow or the stern?, most, if not all people would surely assume a flat squared off shape would be the stern".

George continued, "You know.... I didn't see any real curves at all, it was unlike any other boat that I have ever seen, it looked more like a flat bottomed barge". The team continued to probe for any more details they could obtain. Here, we could wonder why the team had not taken along a special artist of the kind that Police use to get details from witnesses.

"What about the location of the ship George, can you be specific about where it lay on the mountain, were there any specific landmarks?".

George hesitated for a while, then he said, "I do remember that one side of the mountain is impossible to climb, I can recall that my uncle and I went through Bayazit, close to the border, (USSR?) and we climbed the mountain from the direction of Azerbaijan. I can recall seeing many trees and orchards, this would have been somewhere between ten and fifteen thousand feet".

One wonders how George could have known this, he did not say that he had asked his uncle, or that his uncle mentioned it as they climbed. He was only twelve years old, but there may have been some sort of marker to warn climbers regarding the height and to ensure they had oxygen equipment with them because of the thinning of the air. George continued, "We used to pick some of the fruit on our way up there, I'm sure the scenery wouldn't have changed that much, if at all, I could take you right to the spot, but at my age, that might not be too easy".

The team began probing again and brought up the subject of pieces of wood that had been found and whether they could be pieces of the now broken up Ark. In my book, *Pillars of Fire*, Arena Publications, I mentioned religious expeditions that built alters on the mountain using local wood.

George replied to the team, "Listen son, any wood that could be cut would definitely not have come from the Ark, you might try sawing stone with wood tools and see how far you would get. The wood of the Ark had practically turned to stone"...... "Anyway, don't take my word for it, wait until you have found the real Ark, then you will see that there is no connection with all those tales that you hear. The wood that was found was discovered at a much lower level than the position of the Ark".

The investigative team at this point, could have suggested, that if the ship did disintegrate, then some portions of it may have slid down to a lower level, due to some kind of glacial action. However, one would have to see the wood pieces, tested them for hardiness and maybe subject them to the carbon dating process.

When George had stated all of the information that he could recall, he said to the group, "Go, find the Ark, I can't go but you go, I was there seventy years ago, I know it is there".

Bearing in mind, that this interview took place some fifty years ago and practically all of the so-called 'eye witness accounts' regarding the Ark have been de-bunked or explained away as pure fantasy.

However, for all we know, so could the above account by George Hagopian be classified as such. Not that it did not happen, it is well documented, I have seen the P.S.E. print out and still have them. George passed the P.S.E. test and there is no doubt about his apparent sincerity, but the main point on which we could ponder, (not wishing to sound facetious) is why is it, with the wealth of information that has been related, the facts about the description of the Ark, it is fairly precise location, and the routes taken by George and his uncle, that it is not now clearly on display in some maritime museum for all to see?

Nevertheless, the investigative team concluded that George Hagopian's story was sound and that furthermore, it may well be the first fully authenticated eyewitness account on record. Fortunately for George, (if death can be called fortunate) he died shortly afterwards and therefore was spared the stressful ordeal of tolerating the hordes of (what we now call) paparazzi who would have descended on him like locusts, radio and TV reporters, film makers, possibly even a delegation from the Vatican, which would all be quite stressful for an elderly man used to peace and quiet. If George felt, he could not have coped with it all and hid himself away from it all, that would only have made things worse for him. He would be continually looking over his shoulder for someone who may have sniffed out his hiding place. As well as the aforementioned people, a great number of Biblical students would be among them, along with geologists, historians, mountain climbing organisations and many more. If George had his himself away, then the natural assumption would be that George had concocted the entire story and that he was now hiding himself away in order to avoid the embarrassing consequences.

We have said, that the investigating team were satisfied regarding the validity of George's account and went further by saying that all the details that emerged from George's story, fitted very well with the traditions of the Armenian Nation.

We should also mention the other interesting data that the team covered, for example, there is a city called 'Apobaterion' or 'place of departure'. That is, the departure from the area of the Ark, after they had landed by Noah and his group.

During the time of Flavius Josephus, the historian, he gave the city the above name, but it is said that the present name means. 'the place where Noah had landed'. This information is from *The Secrets of the Lost Races*), new English Library.

At one point, the 'old timers', (and there were a lot of them having lived in that healthy environment for many years) would proudly direct enquiring visitors, it is said, to the revered grave site of the Patriarch Noah, and also point out that 'Aghuri', a small town nestled on the slope of the mountain, was the time honoured place, where Noah is thought to have planted his first vineyard.

The Genesis account, being so short on details regarding the actual place where Noah and his family finally emerged from the Ark, is strange, in the fact that it should add in detail regarding Noah being found drunk in his vineyard there by his sons. We will be asking more questions regarding this disembarking process later in another chapter.

There is a document called 'The Table of Nations', that is said to list the descendants of Noah and his children, he had three sons. Later, they all dispersed and travelled widely throughout the world using their vast anti-diluvian knowledge acquired through the centuries, of their existence that patriarchs, such as Noah, had amassed through their century's long lifespans.

Artifacts named 'Ooparts' or 'out of place artefacts', that puzzle science and thus are largely ignored, have been dated as belonging to a technology from long in the past. The great ages of these skillfully manufactured artifacts, that should have required the use of machinery, must be accorded scientific examination and some logical explanation. One of the most significant of these was termed 'the Coso Artefact', which will be described in the next chapter. All these Ooparts, although mind bogglingly ancient, would only have improved in their function down to the ages of the Antediluvians and Noah and his ilk would no doubt have been quite aware of them, perhaps even utilised them.

CHAPTER V

ALL THOSE NOAH'S

Most people are aware that the British and Foreign Bible Society attribute the writings of Genesis to Moses. Genesis, of course, includes the account of Noah and a worldwide deluge that was purposely brought about to cause the destruction of mankind because they had become wicked and degenerate and needed to be disposed of.

I said in *Pillars of Fire*, that this is a little strange in itself, as surely, an infallible divine creative being who was responsible for the creation of humankind, indeed the entire universe ought not to have made mistakes with regard to his human creation programme. We may also add, that 'mistakes' appear to have been made in the somewhat chaotic universe. As the hubble space telescope shows us, that all is not well there either.

However, Moses, whose actual historical existence is disputed by some and is only rooted in ancient Jewish texts as indeed is Abraham, must have been an educated man, after all what better teachers could you have than the Egyptian scribes and Priests?

Nevertheless, Moses could not have been a widely travelled man, as most of his life was spent in the Middle Eastern Regions, either in the house of the Pharoahs or later, in Midian, after he was banished from Egypt. Then of course, his long sojourn in the dessert, after his exodus drama.

Although Moses wrote descriptively about the flood and Noah's Ark, he would not it seems, have had a chance to visit and learn from other nations and their particular Noah legends so, other countries scribes would be busily recording their adventures during and after the flood. Moses never lived to venture anywhere else as he died even before actually reaching Canaan (Israel) after his exodus adventures.

Of course, during his long tuition in the Egyptian education system, he could well have been writing parts of Genesis and would have had access to older Sumerian/Chaldean accounts related to him by the knowledgeable scribes. In the Chaldean culture the name of the person who was their version of Noah, was 'Xisuthros' but in the Sumerian Royal lists, we have Utnapishtim. The suspicion of 'plagiarism' by Moses, is somewhat reinforced by the fact that basically, the same story is written on clay tablets thousands of years before the time of Moses, known as the 'Epic of Gilgamesh'.

So we cannot avoid the fact that Moses could have been well aware of these other versions, certainly the Genesis account is the most widely accepted and known about, but he could have been influenced by the older stories regarding the flood.

Nevertheless, when we consider the many other accounts of the global flood that were well outside the Middle Eastern zones such as China, perhaps we are being a little unfair to Moses.

China had an equal to the hero we know as Noah, the name of the Chinese individual comes as close as it is possible to the Judaic/Christian patriarch in that he was called 'Nu-Wah'.

Importantly to Moses, his hero's boat was not going to be a circular shape, totally unsuitable as a sea-going vessel, but rather a well designed maritime craft fit for oceanic travel. In this regard, it will be shown, that the specific dimensions of Noah's ship, meet with the almost ideal design for oceanic travel and are reflected in the design of modern day vessels.

Just as in the story of Atlantis, an equally enduring story, many different accounts exist of a worldwide deluge and a 'Noah' of their choice. Noah and the anti-Diluvians seemed to have been a highly advanced and knowledgeable people, apparently also scientifically advanced as depicted in all those intricately designed 'ooparts', that were previously mentioned.

Nevertheless, this advanced race and their positive capabilities, were not matched by their behaviour patterns, as they offered themselves by their negative actions as only fit to be destroyed.

The two features of their behaviour do not seem to make sense. One minute sitting at their workbench constructing all those highly advanced ooparts, then going outside to join in all the debauchery, then going back inside to complete their cleverly designed items.

However, there must have been at least a few other 'righteous ones', as well as Noah and his family, alongside all the wicked ones. How did they get along with each other? Just as is reflected today with the rather simple school bully, whose only attribute was the ability to knock others about, such as those (we call nerds) who they envy and punish accordingly. One would expect the 'Noah' types to be equally treated.

However, Noah on the other hand, being as is said is high enough to walk with the Lord', may have overawed the masses. To get to the heart of it, this massive human destruction operation could only be a rather crude form of 'genetic cleansing', in the hope that the few righteous ones would restore the balance in the future generations.

The expeditions, setting out in their attempts to find the historical Ark, on sometimes flimsy evidence, must have at least a few scientists among them in order to evaluate any artifacts or even the Ark itself, in terms of the age and compositions of any discovered items. In the first place, they must believe in the story of the Ark or surely they would not waste their time on such a venture and it follows therefore, that this also implies a belief in the #Divine Retribution' and the whole Genesis story.

This also indicates that scientists are not all hardnosed agnostics or unbelievers, all assuming that the Genesis accounts are simply a fairytale and surely unscientific.

It is said that there are many hundreds of accounts of a worldwide flood saga, written of course, in many different languages, but the Genesis version has made an indelible impression throughout the world.

Although it is scientifically rejected by some as being a worldwide saga, the supposition is quite strengthened by the abundance of legends supporting this from all over the world. However, we cannot deny that there were local flooding events. Nevertheless the wrangle over the issue will most probably always prevail, much like that of Atlantis.

Some researchers have pointed out that the inundation was so absolute, so horrific, that even the highest mountains where inundated with seawater, the Rockies, the Andes, the Himalayas and the Alps bear tell-tale signs, such as clear evidence of oceanic life, seashells, molluscs and so-forth that existed thousands of years also.

Nevertheless, we have already discussed the obvious instability, not only evident in the seabeds but also on the landmasses. Over eons of time, the seabeds and the mountains may have changed places. The Andes are a good example of this 'rapidity' in which the mountains can rise.

At high altitude, we find a fresh water lake, beach sand, and large mooring rings that could accept large sea going vessels. All this indicates the great strength of the tectonic forces where various plates collide against each other in the case of the Andes; it is the force of the 'Nazca' plate heaving against the Peruvian coastline.

The Earth, in any case, is an 'aquatic' world, land masses are seventy-five percent sedimentary. Hardly anywhere on Earth has remained untouched by alluvial forces.

Humans themselves exist in an 'aquatic' environment before birth for nine months, and take to the water with ease. We have all witnessed scenes of young babies swimming with ease and holding their breath under water.

With regard to the worldwide alluvial deposits that have been laid down by millennia due to the action of water, it is said that India has the deepest sedimentary compacted layers thus far, with an incredible depth of sixty thousand feet.

To return to Genesis and the Biblical account of Noah, he was just one of the patriarchs listed by Moses, who tend to prejudice their own credibility as having existed at all, by the incredible amount of years that they lived in comparison to the human with his 'three score and ten'. Although since that phrase appeared (in the Old Testament), human longevity has increased substantially.

In the Fifth Chapter of the Book of Genesis, statistics are given with regard to the lifetimes of the patriarchs. Noah is said to have lived up to the ripe old age of nine hundred and fifty years but his father Lamech only lasted for a mere seven hundred and seventy seven years.

We must ask who was around at the time, to record all these births and deaths so meticulously. Certainly not Moses, what was his source of information? We have said, that Noah was certainly 'unique', or a chosen one as he was described by Moses in Genesis as being high enough to 'walk with the Lord' and even as a child he displayed strange qualities.

The Book of Enoch was once part of the Old Testament but was removed, probably due to its contents. We have to wonder how much more information was removed possibly of a profound nature that may have been more 'scientific' than spiritual because it was 'feared'. The 'censors' and editors over the centuries
may have altered the entire context of the Old Testament and the adventures of the Patriarchs.

The information revealed in the Book of Enoch re-emerged in the Dead Sea scrolls. It relates that Lamech, Noah's father, was somewhat startled by Noah's appearance. His face shone and his eyes 'gleamed' (to use a Biblical expression) Lamech was afraid to come nigh with him, this was when Noah was a child. Such statements as these and others we may not be aware of possibly helped to ensure the 'censors' removed them.

I said in *Pillars of Fire* (Arena Publications) when dealing with the interpretation of the Biblical 'angels' who did not utilise 'wings' but descended on pillars of fire, that the Patriarchs such as Abraham, may have enquired regarding their mission and origins. If he had received a reply such as "We travelled at enormous velocity from the stars to reach your world. Our world has two suns' in the sky". This almost certainly would have been removed by the 'censors'.

To return to the ages of the Patriarchs, Moses was careful not to paint himself into a corner regarding the date of the first man, Adam. If he had been specific, it may have been given the same credibility as a statement by a certain bishop Usher, that the Earth is only four thousand years old and was created on October 23rd at 9.00am (British summer time?). Genesis however, states that Adam lived for nine hundred and thirty years, but omits to tell us from when? Nevertheless, Noah was the Patriarch selected to be the one who would be the saviour of the few and of many other life forms.

Since the construction of a large ship was necessary to accommodate all these worldly creatures and people, one assumes that he must have possessed impressive maritime skills and construction capabilities but no mention of these attributes were made in Genesis, only very basic instructions were given to Noah, mostly with regard to sealing and waterproofing process such as to 'pitch it without and within'. However, the final act of closing up the great door in the Ark was not entrusted to Noah, the Lord himself carried out this task, and the Lord shut him in'. Perhaps it should have read 'shut them in'.

The lighting inside the vessel would have been an important factor, and in my book *Pillars of Fire*, (Arena Publications), I relate how this could have been achieved (certainly not by using firebrands).

When the saga was finally over, and before they left the Ark, there must have been some sort of quick release mechanism designed into the ship so they could emerge. However, in spite of the seemingly rather basic instructions regarding the ships' dimensions, so many cubits long, wide and deep etc., it will be shown that the ship's dimensions were in fact extremely important to the design of a seaworthy vessel and must have been known by either Noah or the Lord himself. Later we will dwell on the whole procedure that must have occurred during the disembarkation and the question of the animals, regarding how they were dealt with and finally dispersed. The actual material that was said to have been used to waterproof the ship within and without is stated as 'pitch'. This is said to mean in Hebrew 'Kopher' thought to mean bitumen or asphalt. This in turn implies that a petroleum-based product was manufactured in large quantities at some location and that this substance was in wide use before the flood.

These factors generate a need to further enquire that products other than sealants must have been widely experimented with. This further implies a sound knowledge of chemistry, mostly in the area of hydrocarbons and the production of other chemically related products such as all kinds of plastics and other synthetic material, machine lubricants and engine fuel etc.

Today, we accept that the word chemistry stems from the word 'Alchemy', but according to the author Rene Noorbergen (Nel Publications) the root word for chemistry is 'Chemia', attributed to 'Khem', which is the ancient name for the land of Egypt. However, we come now to the significance and importance with regard to the seemingly necessary measurements with regard to the aforesaid dimensions of the Ark quoted in cubits. The actual length of the cubit is arbitrary and not 'set in stone', but it is generally accepted as about half a meter or as a 'rule of thumb' (or perhaps we should say arm), that is, the distance between the elbow to the fingertips.

Using this measurement, the dimensions of the Ark would turn out to be (in Biblical terms) three hundred cubits long, fifty cubits wide and thirty cubits high.

In imperial measurements, this would be 450 feet x 75 feet x 45 feet . A photograph taken by a Turkish Air Force pilot flying over Ararat showed a 'ship like' formation, which caused all the interest and ark expeditions as the image photographed fitted roughly these dimensions. As said, the interest was now generated with a wish to confirm whether it was simply a natural rock formation, which (as it happened) turned out to be the case. Nevertheless, some still considered that it may be the petrified remains of the Ark and there was some mention of 'nails'!

However, why was Noah given these specified dimensions, why this particular ratio? The Gilgamesh' epic and its Ark and construction plan seemed totally inadequate for a seagoing vessel, that would have to survive the upheaval and violent sea conditions that would prevail which would require a ship of some stability. The writings of Origen, in his homilies on Genesis, says that he interpreted the Gilgamesh vessel as being a 'boxlike' structure, predominately cubic or hastily designed, that would cause it to turn and spin and would be helpless in any whirlpool conditions.

Nevertheless, the Gilgamesh account of the inundation does resemble the Biblical version in some respects, such as "And when the storm finally came to its end and the terrible water spouts ceased, I opened the window and the light smote my face. I looked at the sea tentatively observing that all humanity had turned to mud and like seaweed. The corpses floated". According to the Genesis versions the Ark rested on the 'mountains' of Ararat, which is a bit different from Mount Ararat, but for centuries Christians have always accepted this location in eastern Turkey, but it is said that Genesis is the only account that mentions this is where the Ark came to rest. Although some historians dispute this, the Turkish
name for the mountain actually means 'Mountain of the Ark' and the Persian (Iranian) name for it is even more specific as it translates as 'The Mountain of Noah'.

So we must ask, why is it that the other accounts regarding their stories, do not make it clear that they agree on this? It does seem strange that their particular hero was not mentioned as landing there. The occupants, when living inside the Ark, would have been in a totally unfamiliar environment than they had been used to, as the ship fought its way along, among the angry waves, it had to endure these conditions for some one hundred and fifty days before coming to rest (as Genesis puts it) on the 'Mountain of Ararat'.

Seasickness would have become routine and the occupants, on arrival, must have been seriously debilitated and also dehydrated, if water rationing had been imposed. The two most similar accounts of the deluge are the Genesis version and the Babylonian Gilgamesh epic.

There are others of course, where the main heroic or 'God like' figure emerges as an important being, attributed to that particular culture.

However, before we analyse the conditions and procedure adopted by Noah and his group after their disembarkation, we must return to the significance and the importance of the specific dimensions that must be followed to build the vessel.

The Bible makes no mention of Noah as being an experienced shipbuilder, or being in possession of a shipyard type of facility, in order to construct the ship, but he was picked out as being qualified for the job.

In the aforementioned 'homilies on Genesis'. The writer assumes that the vessel had a rectangular bottom and that the sides of this ship gradually converged as they rose up, with the top being only one cubic wide. We may recall, that George Hagopian mentioned this in his account , but not such a narrow width on the top. 'Homilies' goes on to say, "Given the conditions resulting from the storm, the fierce rain and the deluge, a more appropriate shape could not have been given for Noah's plan for the Ark. The rain and floodwaters would cascade down the sides from the narrow upper part of the design. The rectangular bottom flat on the water would keep the Ark from pitching under the actions of the wind and waves.

However, it is clear, that the higher authority that gave the specific dimensions to Noah that he must follow, was very knowledgeable in maritime design and of the significance of the particular ratio, that is, its length to breadth ratio being six to one. Obviously even basically, this had a great advantage over the cubic contraption of the Babylonian epic from the standpoint of stability and rolling.

It is stated that the ratio of six to one is about as near perfect as can be desired. Some of the huge seagoing tankers that plough their way through the waves all round the world today, have a ratio of seven to one. The renowned shipbuilder I. K. Brunel, designed the *Great Britain*, an oceangoing liner of 1844. Its dimensions were three hundred and twenty two by fifty one by thirty two and a half feet. Amazingly, these proportions are near identical to the dimensions given to Noah by this higher authority that Genesis accepts as 'God' in order for him to follow for a safe design.

Noah's vessel appears 'suddenly', as though there was nothing to it but Brunel and other shipbuilding moguls had acquired their knowledge of advanced shipbuilding techniques, that had developed and improved over centuries from the earliest basket type coracles building up to the optimum type of design for ocean going voyages. Noah, having got the dimensions right, had many other problems to consider, particularly in regard to the accommodation of the animals and obviously, more importantly, suitable assemblies or cabins for the comfort of his family. One extremely important issue with regard to the interior design, would have to be in the protection of the animals from themselves and the other many varieties, pens, cages, enclosures and so forth so that they would not be thrown about and being made to panic or stampede with fear, as the ship, in spite of any advanced clever design, would bound to lurch about in the conditions described in Genesis, when the flooding was at its height. I mentioned in my book *Pillars of Fire* (Arena Publications) the obvious and profound differences between the stern, vengeful and unforgiving God of the Old Testament and his 'angels', that carried out all the dirty work in Exodus and earlier accounts involving Abraham, Sodom and Gomorrah and so forth, beginning of course with our present issue of killing of most of the human race, are very noticeable, in comparison to the God of the New Testament, with quite the opposite type of policy in how to deal with humanity portrayed in the New Testament, which was concerned with love and forgiveness, turning the other cheek, and loving your neighbours, became the order of the day.

The worldwide annihilation portrayed in the flood epic reads as though it only affected wicked adults but what about the children also destroyed in their thousands. They were not responsible for the actions of their parents, but no doubt, if they were allowed to grow to adulthood, they would have been moulded into the same negative behaviour patterns displayed in their parents.

There is an interesting analogy that emerges here, during the Nazi holocaust and the murdering of all those millions of adults and children could not help but affect the SS guards doing all the annihilating, no matter how hardened Nazi teachings and the SS code had taught them to be. The guards assigned to the task of hauling them off the cattle carts as they arrived and then shepherding them along, what the Nazis called 'the road to heaven', witnessed the old, who were no use for labour, and the children (equally assigned as the same) to their deaths in the gas chambers. It was all very routine and orderly (reflecting planning) but some of the guards where badly affected and traumatised, who may have had young children of their own, and as such required strong counselling. The message instilled into them was "You must remember, that they will grow into adults and then we will have to do this all over again, if we don't, they will become vengeful and rise up against us". such was the depth and ingrained effect of the twisted ideology so well indoctrinated into the minds of the SS recruits, right from their early days in the Hitler Youth, when they where most impressionable.

With regard to the holocaust that Noah was involved in, surely we cannot imagine an equally vengeful God, thinking in these terms. However, it did not stop there, newborn babies of the Egyptian households, where coldly annihilated, prior to the exodus account, such is the aforementioned contrast in policy of the New and the Old Testament accounts.

Nevertheless, Noah and his immediate family, where saved during their particular holocaust. This of course was attributed to the Middle Eastern sector, but as we have said, there were other Noahs. The Chinese version with their Nu-Wah must have found himself ploughing through the South China Sea.

The other leaders or saviours where chosen by other Gods and received their instructions from them. All of this of course, strengthens the supposition of belief that the flood holocaust was a universal event. Was there a Council of the 'Gods' with an agreement made worldwide to carry out the operation? After all, the people of the entire world where seen as only fit to be destroyed (in the Christian version at any rate), that is an awful lot of 'sinning'.

There are factors, such as we have mentioned, that suggest that the biblical flood was universal rather than a traumatic serious local event, but with regard to the Middle Eastern regions, many of the occupants of these areas, were born, lived and died there, even though they may have travelled within these zones. However, it was still 'the world' to them, so one can imagine them believing that it was a worldwide event. The geologist, Hugh Millar, of the nineteenth century, collected worldly traditions of a traumatic nature. Even among the Indians of the Orinoco, a tradition of the worldwide flood inundation is indicated and it was not just prevalent among one specific tribe and was as fresh in their memory as that of the Biblical version is when taught to Judaic/Christian children of today.

Dr Johannes Reim, found flood traditions in Asia, the North American continent, Australia, Europe, Africa and even the South Sea Islands. The common denominator was always the same and seems to indicate that the deluge was indeed universal.

In Hawaiian legends, a certain Nu-u was the righteous one, their God of Destruction was called 'Kane' and instructed Nu-u to save his family by building a great canoe with a house on it. He was also ordered to save all the animals he chose. The comparisons to the Christian account are obvious.

The above edition follows the Genesis accounts quite closely. Regarding the USA there are many Native American Tribes and it is written that forty-six of them have legends of a similar nature that seems to indicate that the deluge was universal. Nevertheless, in his book *Secrets of the Lost Races*, the author points out that resistance to the idea of a worldwide deluge still strongly prevails. However, with all the worldwide stories of an obvious similarity to the Genesis version, this is hard to understand. The written evidence appears to speak for itself in support of the worldwide theory.

Nevertheless, it has been stated that regardless of the profusion of historical indications of a global flood, there are many scientists who steadfastly believe that the Biblical account, the Chaldean account and other deluge stories merely depict local inundations. There has been a constant wrangle between the global versus the local events opinion for decades.

However, the 'local' flood supporters maintain that humanity was still in its infant stage, and therefore emotionally bound to the Middle East, the place of its birth. These scientist reason, that the people were in a sense comparatively primitive, and what was only a local inundation, had them quite sure, that it was a major event that had swallowed up the entire world.

Clearly, these scientists were not of the variety that are baffled and quite concerned that they cannot formulate a clear picture of the antediluvians who where, (shown in the proof of the ooparts) quite technically advanced. There are many that we could mention, but to quote one example, defying any suggestion of primitiveness, in 1961 three rock hunters, Mike Mikesell, Wallace Lane and Virginia Maxey, where collecting geodes in California, on this particular day, when doing a search in the Coso Mountains, they found a stone located near the top of a peak, some four thousand three hundred feet above sea level.

The group thought the stone was a Geode. The following day, when Mikesell cut the stone in half and at the same time ruining a ten inch diamonds saw, he observed that it did not only contain crystals but something totally unexpected. It seemed to be some kind of purposely-manufactured technical device. First, they saw a hexagonal layer of an unknown substance that was softer than agate or jasper. The hexagon shape surrounded a three quarter inch wide cylinder made of solid porcelain or ceramic material and in the centre a two millimeter wide shaft of bright metal.

The artifact was magnetic and showed signs of oxidisation. Circling the ceramic cylinder where rings of copper and these had not corroded. The object was sent to the Charles Ford Society that specialised in analysing extraordinary things. They established that the artifact was indicative of some sort of object that was part of an electrical device.

The closest item one could compare it to would be some kind of 'spark plug' but clearly that was not its function. The rock was found to be around half a million years old. This is only one of the many artifacts or 'ooparts' that science prefers to ignore, simply because there is no explanation for them.

This, and the other objects show that far from being 'primitive' people in their 'infancy' the antediluvians must have been a very advanced race, where the traces of their technical achievements were buried with them under layers of alluvial deposits.

It seems rather a pity that such clever artisans and designers had to exist among the rest that all had to be destroyed. It is hard to imagine how the two distinct qualities could have existed together and how the clever ones where left unmolested to pursue their inventions and advancements. Earthly volcanic upheaval cannot be explained for all of the 'ooparts', that is, when geological disturbance may cause them to fall to a lower level, where the Earth was rent asunder, rather like the San Andreas fault, then later found due to the digging process then dated wrongly when analysing nearby organic matter. This could indeed occur but as said, there are too many of them to accommodate this theory.

There is a strange anomaly to consider here when some of the ooparts are discovered due to deep excavations, or blasting out quarry rock etc., OK, we are mystified at their great age, but we assume that they are at this depth because of all the millennia of earthly material that has covered them. How then is it possible to find dinosaur bones that often appear 'themselves' due to wind erosion that are sixty five million years old?

They are so close to the surface after all this time, should this not raise questions? They died (so we believe) all that time ago, yet are still on the surface. A skeleton of a stray cow that died just days ago that had been picked clean by predators and its bones bleached in the Desert sun on some remote Texas ranch could be quite explainable but next to it, wind erosion may cause a bone to be sticking out of the ground that proved to be sixty five million years old when analysed, surely a curious thing?

However, the 'Cosovo' object that was found on a high mountain, inside a Geode, was obviously not of the 'deeply buried' type which seems to indicate that 'ooparts' can show up anywhere but the accuracy in dating them must be paramount.

With regard to the immense ages of the Patriarchs such as Noah, we have said that Genesis carefully avoids mentioning the date of Adam's birth alleged to be the first man, but is quite lucid in detailing the life spans of the other Patriarchs. From these, we could calculate roughly the time of Adam's birth.

Genesis tell us that Cain, Adam's son, was born in 4969 BC and died in 4059 BC, so Adam, who was said to have lived for nine hundred and thirty years and being the father of Cain would have to have been born sometime around 5,000 BC.

However, just to be discussing these factors, puts us in the same group of people who reverently accepted bishop pushers calculations, that the Earth is only four thousand years old and was created on October 23rd. Of course, science and the age of enlightenment destroyed all his calculations that where arrived at. For the creation of the Earth, based on the ages of the Patriarchs listed so 'matter of factly', in Genesis.

However, today, no ecclesiastical college of Biblical students would accept that Adam was created along with the universe and the Earth, at such a date. Surely this puts us in the same position, when believing in the possible existence of a petrified hulk of the Ark of Noah and indeed of Noah himself, in that it would necessitate a belief in Genesis, the creation, and the wrath of God scenario that would have caused the petrified Ark to be there in the first place, yet organised expeditions still set off to search for it.

However, as for the actual ages of the Patriarchs as quoted, and of longevity in general, as a topic, they deserve closer scrutiny and analysis, which we will deal with in due course. As wicked, as the antediluvians were said to be the 'creator' ensured that none survived in the Middle Eastern zones or the rest of the world for that matter. Regarding the mass annihilation except those chosen by God, (or the Gods), when assigning all the other equivalents to our Biblical Noah. We are conditioned to believe in the worldwide inundation; therefore, everyone in the world must have been assessed as wicked, except of course for the chosen ones. This of course brings us back to the question of a divine infallible God and how he could have made such a mistake in creating humanity, only later being seen fit only to be destroyed.

However, 'God' or the gods, certainly found the task of controlling the necessary weather conditions quite easy, they also employed their skills in stopping the deluge when they decided that the time was right to do so and all the wicked ones had died.

In my book *Pillars of Fire*, when touching on the flood saga, I mentioned that Genesis made it quite clear that the gods 'stopped', 'restrained' and 'halted' the flood just as easily as they started it. The evidence of worldwide horrors is shown in the rapid end to millions of marine species, showing that the flood was ferocious and rapid. This is borne out by the geological analysis of almost immediate silting, with huge amounts of alluvial deposits that trapped millions of fish and very quickly entombed them in complete skeletal form.

This of course, was the initial phase of fossilisation, where today they can be seen in rock with all their bones completely in place.

There was no chance of any other predatory sea creatures being able to devour them, as they had expired along with all the others and this point is well taken, when discussing whether or not the flood was worldwide and catastrophic. These factors cannot be denied, yet amazingly, they are. Of course, a worldwide inundation could have nothing to do with Genesis at all, but the significant factor is the lack of a gradual process of inarticulation and natural breakup and dispersal of the bones. Their deaths were immediate and sudden. Billions of fish died in agony, portrayed in their body forms, contorted, curved and contracted, with the tail, in many circumstances bent around the head, indicating that they died in convulsions.

Many legends from around the world speak of the ferocity of the deluge. For example the Maya, in their sacred book, *The Chilam Balam*, a passage states, "In one great watery blow came the waters and the sky fell down". In my book, *When the Moon Came*, (Arena Publications) I offered a theory that was based on the calculations of George F Dodwell, regarding the lurching of the Earth from an almost vertical position to twenty six and a half degrees, and then some time later rolling back again to its present position of twenty three and a half degrees.

We may know more about the changing of the Earth's axis and the obvious turmoil and flooding that would have occurred on Earth, if a will through religious zeal by destroying people's historic records had been matched by a wish to preserve them.

A shameful destruction of many Mayan codices was carried out, where only portions remain.

The Maya also described in their 'Chilam Balam' that when the sky fell down, 'the dry land sank', which may of course have been the waters coming up rather than the land sinking. It goes on to say "And in a moment, the great annihilation was finished". The Maya were meticulous recorders of detail but it was just the same in other parts of the world, rare and priceless documents were destroyed through human ignorance and superstition of anything seen as a threat to their religious works. The possible capture of the Moon, said to have occurred around 12,000 BC, may have caused the first conflagration then a couple of thousand years later lurching back once again to the twenty three and half degrees figure we know of today. As said, earlier, when considering George F Dodwells calculations, the gravitational effects of the Earth would have caused the second inundation and may explain the Biblical flood and possibly the loss of Atlantis as we discussed in that particular chapter. However, the Earth could never return to its near vertical position due to the gravitational effects of the captured Moon, although some recent reports and calculations suggest that it might be trying to do so.

Now let us examine, in logical terms, the chain of events leading up to the time of the departure of Noah and his family. Having wondrously constructed this ship, the size of an ocean going liner. Obviously Noah and his family must have 'shone out' in their behaviour, in comparison to the rest of the masses, who where only seen fit to be destroyed. This surely would have generated some resentment and jealousy among the local residents who had been frequently warned to repent and to reject their wicked ways, which, of course, they all ignored to their peril.

Further resentment would have been generated by Noah being seen as fit to 'walk with the Lord'. Noah could not have built this huge boat in a couple of weeks so a gradual resentment and dislike of Noah would have prevailed. Much whispering and gossip would have simmered away, regarding what he was up to, for example, "Who is this goody two shoes, who thinks he is such a cut above the rest of us?" Things would only have got worse, when they saw all the animals being shepherded into the Ark.

It is necessary to analyse here, this whole saga of the animals and their various types. It was not only Noah and his family that where earmarked for survival, Noah had to save two of every species of all the other creatures on the Earth in order to get things back to normal later. Did he save snails, sharks, snakes, whales? How could be possibly have achieved this? Not all species lived in the assumed Middle Eastern zone of departure. Genesis avoids any mention of the problems that would have faced Noah in this regard. He would have had to travel around the world with an experienced group of trappers and all the necessary cages and methods of containing them all and getting them back to the Ark.

We must consider the lions, panthers, tigers, giraffes, elephants, bears, crocodiles, alligators, rhinos, hippos and many others. A tremendous ordeal for him and his team, particularly if it was only his sons that helped him.

This would obviously have been just as great a challenge as his construction of the vessel and all the necessary compartments to house them. Nevertheless, we have to believe that he did accomplish it, if we are to believe the story at all.

As said, when the envious crowd saw the animals going in two by two, they would have put two and two together and most certainly, it would be the last straw when seeing the great doors being closed up. We have said that this task was not entrusted to Noah and was carried out by the Lord himself. Genesis states "And the Lord shut him in". If the crowd had harboured any notions of rushing the vessel and scrambling up the gangway to save themselves (as they would now firmly believe all the warnings), the Lord would no doubt be able to deal with them.

However, they would be finally convinced that they were doomed, when they saw the skies darkening and marble sized raindrops falling increasingly all around them. There would have been pandemonium outside, when the crowd would obviously in their panic surge forward and begin yelling, shouting and hammering on the sides of the vessel and in doing so could have disturbed the ship if large enough numbers attacked, even maybe knocking it off its moorings or rather support beams.

All of this would have greatly disturbed all the animals inside the ship. In the event, clearly nothing happened, but the animals would still have been affected by fear, when all the rocking and surging of the flood waters really took hold and unless the ship had been suitably designed within to restrain them. The boat would have been difficult to control but Noah seemed to manage it. Perhaps the animals were prevented from surging about. So obviously, a lot of thought went into the interior design. The higher power that organised all of this 'escape strategy' when deciding to murder all their faulty creations, must (as said) be responsible for making mistakes in their creation of the faulty humans, in the first place, implying that the creator was not an infallible being.

It must be said, that the 'final solution' of the annihilation of the masses, did not entirely work with regard to the continual negative behaviour patterns of the human, that he and his sons had produced over the centuries of this continual longevity of Noah in his long lifespan of nine hundred and fifty years.

The despots, villains and murderers of other humans, still prevailed in later years. The Herods, Caligulas, Neros, who in their turn, did their share in the slaughter of the innocents, particularly Nero, who delighted in watching the slaughter of the 'righteous' sect known as the Christians, by being torn to pieces by lions in the arena, in order to amuse him and his friends.

Nevertheless, because of the firm beliefs of the Christians in going to their deaths in their thousands, indicates some success in many humans like them who accepted death instead of renouncing their faith? In any case, humans had been given an excess of 'a grey matter' by the creator (or possibly creators) so that humans themselves will eventually solve the issue of positive and negative behaviour by the necessary scientific advancements and discovery of how the brain works, with neuronal research and eventually laying bare the entire human genome to be manipulated in the positive mode and eliminating the negative and bringing all of the complexities of the human under human control.

Already, genes have been discovered that govern intelligence, will it be any more difficult to identify and isolate those genes that govern negative behaviour? Earlier we mentioned a case where Mellon Thomas Benedict in a N.D.E had been told by an entity or 'being of light', that humans had always possessed the power to heal themselves and this will surely come to pass.

However, to return to the subject of Noah and his Ark, when they finally disembarked from the Ark, just as many questions must be asked as in the departure preparations. Those that emerged from the Ark, were the last of the antediluvians who possessed those enormous life spans, so they were not in a hurry to go among the carnage below where they waters had receded and the horror that was left behind would have been obvious.

Far better to wait for nature to clear things up and readjust itself. Now we must analyse the whole process of the disembarkation and its associated problems. When the great door was opened and they emerged into their new environment, they would have to ensure that none of the creatures inside got out or escaped prematurely, until the survivors were ready to release them in a controlled and orderly fashion.

One would imagine that the first creatures to be allowed to escape would be the fierce variety. First the tigers, panthers, cheaters, lions and forth. They would quickly depart and not hang around like pets waiting for be fed; they were quite used to doing that for themselves. Once these 'fleet of foot' creatures had quickly dispersed, they would get rid of such animals as the bears, who would one supposes, lumber away fairly quickly.

After that, one could assume that it would be the turn of the slower creatures such as the giraffes and elephants, and so forth. One thing they would not be short of would be a good supply of fuel for their fires and the construction of their dwellings. This of course, would be the material used to construct all the pens and enclosures, within the Ark, namely wood. To restrain and prevent the domesticated creatures, they would have to rebuild all the pens, enclosures and corrals to accommodate their horses, cows and goats, sheep and chickens so they had a practically unlimited supply of food, wool for clothing, horses for ploughing and so forth. Chickens for their eggs and for food.

They would not be too badly off at all, and as some of the creatures on the ship during the one hundred and fifty day voyage, would have procreated; quite to the advantage of the group, only the variable climate would be their enemy.

However, since we are told in Genesis, that Noah had constructed a vineyard, the climate in their area, would surely have been temperate enough to produce grapes. That they were successful in this is the additional snippet in Genesis that Noah's sons had found him drunk there.

STRANGE REALITIES

But eventually, it would be time to leave in order to carry out the work they were saved for in the first place, which one supposes, would have been similar to that which Adam, the first Patriarch received which was to 'Go forth and replenish the Earth".

With the huge lifespans attributed to them, they would have had plenty of time to do so. When the 'Ark hunting' era began, which would have increased after the story of George Hagopian, the locals could exploit the story and they would have been able, if they wished, to profit from the story of Noah and the relationship with their homeland, and they did so. Noah would not have lived and died in the area, but would have eventually moved on, as we said, but this did not prevent the 'old timers' directing Ark hunters and tourists to the revered graveside of Noah. One wonders what an exhumation may reveal, if not considered, sacrilegious. This venture may just be (in modern parlance) 'a nice little earner' for the locals. Historic sites are always replete with souvenirs' and gift shops and anything related to it that may be sold to the tourists.

Nevertheless, the locals may be right when directing visitors/tourists, to Noah's vineyard at 'Aghuri' and Genesis does, as we have said, state that Noah did construct one, but he certainly would not have remained in the vicinity of Ararat and where the Ark was alleged to have come aground. Noah lived for some hundreds of years after leaving the Ark and it is written that the survivors saw it as their mission to regenerate the Earth.

However, as said, if there is a graveside there, it would be interesting for this to be further investigated. With regard to his vineyard, one wonders if a vineyard could flourish in such weather conditions that prevail up in the mountains. We are conditioned to believe that vineyards prefer warm sheltered areas and the continental effects that such countries as France, Italy, Spain, South Africa, and Australia experiences.

It brings to mind an amusing comment by the actor in a film where he is showing off with his knowledge of wines, "If grapes get too much of the Dordogne wind, they have a tendency to sulk".

Of course, Noah and his descendants, when moving through the new world on their travels, would have had many choice areas to pick from, if they wished to plant any more vineyards.

When it comes to analysing the whole story of Noah, as per Genesis, many people accept it word for word, why else would there be so much interest in Ararat. In addition, forming ark-searching expeditions. There are people who accept the entire Bible and its teachings, but surely with some reservations? However, as we have said, to accept the stated ages of the Antediluvian Patriarchs, is another matter and remains an Enigma. Adam, the first man, is said to have lived for nine hundred and thirty years, Seth for nine hundred and twelve years, Enos nine hundred and three years, it continues on the Lamech, Noah's father, whose lifespan dropped back to seven hundred and seventy seven years, but this was not a downward trend, for, as we have said, his son Noah lived for nine hundred and fifty years. Nevertheless, one would not expect there to be any scientific support for the stories but the opposite is the case.

Dr Hans Selye, one time Director of the Institute of Experimental Surgery of Montreal University says, "Medicine has assembled a fund of knowledge that will now serve, I believe, as a point of departure for studying the causes of old age. If the causes of old age can be found, there is no good medical reason to believe that it wouldn't be possible for scientists to find some practical way of slowing down the process gradually or even bringing it to a standstill.

Most people are aware, that all the features and processes of the human body have a gene or group of genes that control everything in the development of the human. When we have discovered the entire human genome, genes that control everything could themselves be controlled by humans.

Rene Noorbergen (*Secrets of the Lost Races*) states, "There are numerous factors that may have contributed to the longevity of the Biblical Patriarchs indeed, all of modern humans early predecessors.

Originally, man was undoubtedly possessed with considerably more vitality than we have today, or he would not have been victorious in the struggle for survival. Scientific discoveries lead us to believe that the pre-flood world of the antediluvians had a more agreeable climate than today and areas that are now deserts once blossomed and tropical flora once grew in the Polar Regions.

This is borne out to some degree when we can observe cave drawings in the parched Sahara showing hunters stalking their prey in pastoral scenes. Plants once thrived in rich virgin soil but the raging seething waters of the deluge churned up the top layer of the Earth's crust, tearing the fertile layers away and washing and eroding them down to the sea, with only a fraction of the nutrients needed for human well being left. Today, many people rely on vitamin pills for their health. The ancients may have been well aware of all the necessary herbs and advantageous things to eat regarding health in general, including longevity. As it is, the human lifespan is continually increasing and has risen to the point where people living to a hundred years of age is fairly common place today, almost as though the body is trying to recover longevity.

Given that the human lifespan has almost doubled since the Roman occupation of Britain, that we ended around 400 AD, then if it was to continue at that rate then in the year three thousand people should be living to around two hundred years or more, that is, if other forces beyond our control kindly let us live, which they may not have made their mind up about yet.

There is a scientific opinion that man may have existed for millions of years longer than the science of geology, archaeology and anthropology currently accept.

This is reinforced to some degree by the really ancient objects that reflect technical design and the existence of craftsmen and advanced engineering processes that must have existed so long ago, it is almost unbelievable, yet there they are, sometimes found embedded in stone, reflecting the 'ancientness' of the designers.

Bjorn Kurten in *Not from the Apes* says, "Recent discoveries have revealed the disconcerting fact (for anthropology), that the basic human has always existed, not as an offspring of apes but as a man since time immortal".

Some humans for various reasons degenerated from the human stock and as a result, are believed to be a less evolved human slotted into the necessary timeframe.

It has been possible in recent times to demonstrate that the human lineage can be followed back into far more distant times, where it still retains its unique character. As a result, we may doubt that our ancestors could every properly be called an ape.

All this makes sense, zoologically, as the contrasts between apes and men in anatomy, are two great to be reconciled with a relatively recent origin.

All of this seems to indicate that the amazing longevity of Noah and of course, the other Patriarchs may not be so unbelievable after all.

The Bible, in particular, the Old Testament, seems to be a document to be either totally rejected or totally accepted, rather than isolating various texts and passages into those, which we like, or those we do not accept.

However, a document, such as the Old Testament, that is said to have first appeared in its basic form in AD 70 has lasted long enough for us to assume that some texts may be based on truth or even events that did actually occur, but recorded details purposely removed.

To return to Noah and the Patriarchs and their extreme longevity, a graph, compiled and included in 'medical science' and the Bible (William R. VIS) shows an enormous drop in longevity after Noah. Some will say, "Of course, because they never had such longevity in the first place, and/or can we be one hundred percent sure that Noah even existed?" All valid points.

Nevertheless, the conditions on Earth in the post Diluvian period, after the ravages of the flood, would be, in comparison to the 'Utopian' conditions enjoyed by Noah and the 'pre-flood' population, extremely unfavourable.

We could offer a comparison here, to our first chapter, dealing with the Comte St Germain with Noah no longer having access to the necessary herbs and potions made from them for his version of 'an elixir of life' that may have been taken for granted in his pre-flood existence and grew all around him for the taking.

After all, if the ancients were so clever to have produced all those amazing artifacts (ooparts) other branches of science and medicine may have been equally advanced.

But Noah and his descendants, when travelling the Earth and assisting the survivors (there are always survivors) and instructing them in many things, may have passed into some earthly legends who viewed them as 'gods' among men, and this scenario is reflected in many ancient written works that have survived. Even more enlightening records may have been purposely destroyed along with many other documents. If there were no survivors who would have recorded all the drama? The ancients that did contribute to the historical documents pertaining to their race and their culture, were certainly impressed enough by these 'teachers' or demi-gods in order to take the trouble to record it all.

The Maya, in their sacred book the Popul Vuh stated, "The first men possessed tremendous knowledge of the world, they were able to know all and they examined the four corners of the world and the four points of the arch of the sky (the cardinal points N.S.E and west) and the round face of the Earth".

Here, we have an ancient people making it clear that they knew the Earth was a sphere, when even in the time of Columbus, many people where quite convinced that the Earth was flat.

When we consider our own myths and historical writings referring to God 'gods' and demi-gods, we would have to include the Old Testament among them, but the fact is, the ancient legends of the Maya and others, make more sense than the first chapters of Genesis reflecting on creation of the firmament, the Earth and humanity all within a week and that the first humans, that is, Adam and Eve, appearing as fully evolved and developed humans in 5000 BC, but this is a dilemma for the ecclesiastics and those who study Biblical date to come to terms with.

However, the story of Noah and the flood is firmly entrenched therein (and indeed, all over the world), but that is only one aspect of Genesis. It is hard to believe that any logical thinking scientists or scholars could ever accept the story of creation as it is written in the Judaic/Christian account. Yet for all that, the belief still remains. Even astronauts, who mostly are scientifically minded and academically qualified, quote the writings of Genesis and creation from space. Certainly, from their viewpoint when seeing the beautiful blue earth suspended in space, it is certainly an overawing sight and tends to stir belief in some higher power, even a divine creator.

With regard to another work (and there are many of them) it says, "Until the time of the eighteenth century, very few historians, academics and scholars, doubted the accuracy of the Biblical stories. Even the creation event and the story of the flood and the Sojourn of the Israelites in their lengthy desert wanderings after exodus. It seemed to them, that all these events where factual.

Then everything changed, along came the infamous 'age of reason', now, the once solid walls of faith where breached. This of course, was the coming of the nineteenth century that brought with it, so many new ideas, theories that upended the well-established belief in divine creation.

There is no doubt, that these new theories of evolution and other challenges, to views once accepted only through 'blind faith', where most disturbing to the ecclesiastical fraternity and even to science.

This new enlightened and materialistic era, ensured that many of the stories and especially the historical Biblical accounts were relegated to mythology and many people began to regard the entrenched Biblical accounts as little more than well-contrived compilations or fables.

Yet for all that, and in quite a contrast, it has now been said, that some 'modern' historians, although not accepting every part of the Bible as literal fact, they have come to accept that much of the Biblical data seems to constitute an unusually reliable historical document of antiquity. Often, this is reflected in archaeological discoveries in the parts of the world where the alleged stories and events took place. One example is the convincing battle involving Jericho and the formidable dimensions of the walls that the Israelites had to overcome, when breaching the walls of the city, as they appeared so indestructible. Another example was the discovery of the ancient birthplace of the Patriarch Abraham namely, Professor William F Albright, a renowned archaeologist, late of John Hopkins University, Baltimore, USA , seems to view the Bible, taken as a whole, as partly acceptable.

"Its languages, the life, events and customs of the people, its history, with its ethical religious ideas are all quite illustrated in innumerable ways by clear archaeological history and its discoveries".

There are others, of course, who will say that this view and these kind of statements only reflect and deal with the general life of the Middle East and its people existing in those times and does not really seem to contribute any validation to the sometimes 'mind stretching' texts and Biblical accounts.

In a sense, this is true as even today, in some areas, life among the peoples continues in the same way as it did in Biblical times. Arabs riding camels, others herding sheep and goats, living in tents, eating the same food as so forth.

However, the data regarding a Noah and the patriarchs contained in Genesis, with regard to their births, deaths, how long they lived and so forth is quite specific and is written as though there is no doubt of its validity.

The ages of the Patriarchs going back to the first man Adam, who the Old Testament tells us, lived for nine hundred and thirty years but as said, does not tell us from when? However, we have estimated at around 5000 BC yet ancient dwellings older than this date have been found. Dates regarding the other patriarchs are firmly quoted down to the actual year of their deaths who could possibly verify this date. But when reviewing the said data, it all seems to have occurred around 3000 BC to 5000 BC, but Adam's birth date shows that Moses must have been using this chronology somewhere near our estimate of 5000 BC Adams sons Cain and Seth were said to have been born in 4909 and 4924 respectively.

Nevertheless, none of the explicit detail, although mysterious, with regard to its origin as really matters when we must continually face up to the everlasting question of who is right? With regard to the science versus the Genesis, story.

From the various quotes that exist, and the few we have mentioned, made by scholars who have pondered the question, it is clear that the question is far from resolved and that some members of the various sciences do not discard entirely the validity of some of the Biblical texts, but those generated in the earliest accounts by Moses for example in his Genesis story must remain questionable.

We have asked can there be any logical thinking scientist who could accept the creation of everything in seven days. Even if science is wildly out in its estimate of the beginning of creation, that is the so called 'big bang' (which may not have been a 'bang' at all) by even a few billion years. The process of it remains the same in the assumption that the actual date of it is not settled by any means and seems to be quite flexible. This is true, of course, with any theories and assumptions regarding the cosmos and textbooks that seem so sure of astrophysical theories and data have to be continually revised or even declares as obsolete. There is nothing more true than the statement "The universe is not only stranger than we imagine; it is stranger than we can imagine".

However, with regard to Noah, the ancient Patriarchs Adam and Eve and all the rest of the often-disputed data in Genesis, science itself as we have said, has often to be quite flexible and not remain rigidly fixed in original beliefs and estimates. The date of scientific creation is currently in a downward mode.

Even if the creation of the Earth took place twelve billion years ago instead of the former estimate of twenty billion, and the currently accepted age of four and half billion years for the creation of our solar system is correct, neither of these dates could have witnessed the arrival on Earth of the anatomically modern human entity that would be considered as preposterous.

However, Genesis clearly states that a divine God created the universe and everything in it at the same time. This of course would sit better and be more acceptable if it did not include the creation of man, but it does, which falls immediately into the hands of cynical scientists guided by logic, and Moses, who is attributed as the author of the creation event, obviously prejudiced his own credibility by stating such, and even if he had left it out or attributed it to a much later date, questions would still be asked, why did God wait for so long after his major work of creation to produce humans?

Yet even if he had, it would be asked, after such a long period of time, why did he get it so wrong with regard to humans, who had to be wiped out except for Noah and his family (plus the animals of course). After all, he did get it right with Noah and all the other Patriarchs.

Although the anthropologists are continually pushing back their estimates for the appearance of anatomically modern humans, they have absolutely no hope of ever having it go so far back to accord with the Biblical creation stories. It could be assumed, that as the onset of cultural evolution accepted by the anthropologists as commencing some forty thousand years ago, that if we add on another ten thousand or so years a good estimate for the anatomically modern, creative, thinking human would be around fifty thousand years ago. Of course, humans in modern form may go back further in time, but just existed as reapers mowers and agricultural beings living in basic dwellings and carrying on that way for millennia as did the pre-Columbian folk, but the beginnings of the great intellects, philosophers, mathematicians and those contributing to the advancement in medical science, are the result of the cultural evolution, almost as though humanity was given a boost (perhaps genetically by a different creator) to reach the level of advancement we enjoy today.

However, who is to say that this was not achieved much earlier than we think in regard to Noah and the advancements of the antediluvian people?

When we work through the list of the earliest Patriarchs down to Noah, he is the one who stands out above all the others and stamped his name into history, where, even today, in our assumed enlightened age, people still assemble teams to search for the remnants of his mystical Ark, and certainly highly reinforced by our previous and rather convincing story of George Hagopian, not only visiting the Ark but climbing on to it.

CHAPTER VI

MY CARBON FOOTPRINT

Before the first proto-humans were around, there was no humans handy to take the blame for our climate's erratic behaviour patterns, which still prevail and always have done. If people where around two hundred and fifty million years ago, they would have had to endure a major catastrophic event when ninety-five percent of all earthly species where wiped out. It is postulated that the solar system, during the galactic merry-go-round could have passed through an area of the galaxy containing high quantities of cosmic dust and gas, perhaps causing another ice age or the lowering of the Sun's heat reaching Earth. The galaxy takes approximately two hundred and fifty million years to rotate, this means we are now back at the same point (oh dear).

This could be a little disturbing (if we bothered to worry about it), when I pointed out that there was no one around to take the blame for the above mentioned calamity, now of course, there is. The Government's coffers are filling up nicely with all the green taxes that are levied. The Earth has always regulated itself and science knows it. We could be simply warned with regard to certain things we should not do, to recycle, to use low emission fuels and so forth, but there would be no money in that, humans have to be made aware that is all our fault.

People in these times have enough to worry about without being pressured about climate change, but realise that it is best to comply in order not to aggravate the situation, but Government funded scientific institutions vie with each other to make the worst dire predictions. As soon as the 'buzz words' carbon footprint where formulated one could hardly turn on the TV or buy a newspaper without encountering them, and all the dire warnings of what humans are doing to the world. We began to be slowly but surely laden with shame and guilt about it all and became easy to convince that due to our careless behaviour we will have to pay for it.

The people of the Earth and of course all the pollution caused by industrial factories, which humans were responsible for, were actively shovelling carbon into the atmosphere by the bushel.

The trees must have been very frustrated in that they could not talk, if they could they would shout out in full volume "Wait a minute, why don't you ask us, we love it, bring it on, don't let us diminish, then we and the food producing plants will flourish for you".

One may recall, that not too long ago, the media, TV networks and newspapers where warning with earlier buzzwords, 'Ice Age imminent'. Dire warnings about another ice age, but then, I do not recall the science fraternity getting away with blaming humanity for it.

Whatever calamity that is alleged to be soon upon us, they all seem to be intent on causing the people of the Earth to become neurotic worriers and paranoid about it, this of course, is why many people take little notice anymore, regarding Doomsday, it has prophesised itself out of existence.

Nevertheless, we cannot simply switch off and forget about it all. Very few would argue, that the Earth is perfectly all right and the same as it ever was is to deny the scientific facts. The most annoying fact is that humanity always has to take the blame. Sure, we have contributed to it, but our efforts are puny compared to nature, the Earth is and was quite capable of cooling and warming itself without any help from humans at all. For example, what if all the volcanoes that are present around the Pacific 'ring of fire' decided to erupt in unison. Of course, (we hope) this is geologically impossible, from what science think it knows about the turbulent workings of the inner Earth.

However, if we return to the allegations that we are smothering the Earth will all this additional carbon one might start to consider that we may have to have a re-think about the gasses that make up the atmosphere of the Earth. Originally, our physics lessons taught us that the one hundred percent volume of the atmosphere of the Earth is comprised of seventy eight percent nitrogen (which is said to give us our blue sky) then twenty one percent oxygen and one percent of 'other gasses', which of course includes carbon.

Now, we cannot mess around with the one hundred percent volume and keep the proportions as quoted above 'in balance' as it where, if we increase the one percent portion of the 'other gases! The nitrogen and oxygen would have to be reduced accordingly in order to keep the one hundred percent volume correct.

So where does all this leave us? Except to ask of science, may we be informed of the new percentages? I thought that the only way I could get an answer to this could be to put it to the public through my local newspaper in the hope that some person or scientific outlet would enlighten me.

A response was received in the same Editor's column but it was not considered satisfactory. It seemed to skirt around the subject, the bottom line being "It doesn't work like that". However, just how it did work was not explained.

This alleged abundance of additional carbon and what it could do to the environment witnessed the birth of the 'greenhouse gas' issue. We are hurriedly converting the Earth into Venus. Whereas these prophets of doom always concentrate on the negative issues, they never seem to even consider any beneficial factors such as we have mentioned, with the trees and the food producing plants. With regard to the fact that we are concreting over a large portion of the globe then any additional carbon may help to restore the balance so to speak. We have lost a huge volume of oxygen that would have been emitted by all these decimated trees, which brings us back to our question regarding the 'percentages' dilemma and our atmosphere.

Obviously, anyone with any sense of the precious nature of the environment, is concerned about the 'greenhouse gas' issue, but critics will say "Of course you are, this is precisely what is intended, green issues have helped to develop a multimillion pound enterprise.

The largest countries, USA, China and so forth, with their huge industrial output bear the most criticism, and this is how it should be, if they do not sign up to worldwide agreements on actions to control it. Nevertheless, the fact remains that we do see profiteering all around us. One small component is that when you take your car in for an oil change you are now charged a fee to cover the cost of the disposal of the old oil, which may not be 'disposed' of at all but recycled into a product sold for profit.

Scientists and climatologists, who are the ones that study the subject intently, with regard to records, going far back into the past are well aware of the known fluctuations that have occurred over the millennia. If asked about the constant warnings we are subject to regarding 'climate change' they really ought to respond, or could do so, by saying, "So what's new?" However, they do not, they will add to the worries of anyone enquiring of the about the climate problem by reinforcing the belief that it is a 'big issue'.

Any scientific students leaving university bursting with knowledge and clutching their Degrees have overcome their first hurdle. Now they are confronted with a second hurdle and it is a big one finding a job.

Scientific institutions are restricted by their overheads and expenses and like any business venture, they have to stay within their (profit margins in business) budgets and Government grants. They can be or have to be somewhat selective in who they accept as an 'employee'. Clearly, those Graduates who have 'shone' in university will have the best chance.

Most people are or should be glad that we do have these organisations working hard to prevent us from totally damaging the environment, with our polluting emissions of varying kinds. On the other hand, many people began to see through their subterfuge in having us believe that things are much worse than we imagined. For example, the Arctic conditions of heavy snow continually packing down on former layers has to make its way somewhere if possible. It does so by the glacial factor.

The snow sheets slide slowly down to the sea and form the ice cliffs, these eventually drop off in great slabs into the sea, but rather than explain that it is a natural process, the inference is, that it is all caused by humans, who have created the climate change problem due to excessive heating, that is now causing this effect. It is a fact that some of the Arctic is melting, but film shots are shown when the warmer season is in force, where natural melting would occur anyway. If there is a real problem then they ought to come clean about it and omit the subterfuge.

If we go back to our recently employed student, who has to be paid a salary, the cash to pay their employees must continue to come in, in the form of Government grants. Therefore, these institutions must try to raise their profile at all costs, this is the root cause of the subterfuge. Often alarmist and sometimes-exaggerated statements are made, to draw attention to their institution and ensure the grants keeping coming in.

Nevertheless, we should be glad they are there and doing their best to protect our environment. Science is also fully aware that climate change has fluctuated over the millennia. This is made clear to them when analysing the tubes of material broken up into segments indicating the varying time period of the past.

These core samples are obtained by deep core drillings of the Ocean beds and various other places on the Earth, including the ice caps. When studying the segments they have found that the magnetic field of the Earth has also fluctuated over the centuries as well as the world's temperature. They can tell this by analysing the small particles and determining their north south orientations.

These ecological changes were taking place long before the earliest humans lit their campfire and so could not become the scapegoats to take the blame for it all.

With the advancements of science, we are all naturally more aware of the dangers we can cause to the environment, but not so much, perhaps, at the onset of the industrial revolution. Certainly, we were quite aware of the effects but not what these effects may be doing to the environment and the long-term results for our offspring at the time, who could not be aware, especially if living in or near an industrial town? The large number of tall chimneys belching out all that thick smoke and of course the mass of carbon. Huge factories and the 'dark satanic mills' were everywhere. Humans did not like it but where less inclined to worry about it, as most of them earned their living from it. These conditions prevailed all over the industrial towns of Britain, largely in the north west of Lancashire and east, in the Yorkshire mill towns.

STRANGE REALITIES

It was the medical profession, largely when dealing with the more serious cases of silicosis in the miners, that if so much carbon was being ingested by the workers underground. How much of it was made being taken into the lungs by this soot (carbon) above the ground , at that time worse by the fogs, when holding it in became known as 'smog' and it was obviously a problem that was injurious to health. Just as in the days of cigarettes, before the introduction of filters one could blow the exhaled smoke through a white handkerchief and observe the brown deposits of nicotine that was being deposited into the lungs. This was also clearly observed when holding a handkerchief in front of the face, when struggling through the thick smog. The handkerchief was black with soot that would have otherwise gone into the lungs, something certainly had to be done.

In less, damp or foggy weather the particles that rained down on the town and its people, then became known as 'smuts' (a derogative of the German word Schmutzig, meaning 'dirty').

These effects where particularly noticeable to the proud housewife, competing with her neighbours to produce the whitest nappies and sheets on their clothes lines and also a curse, in the absence of washing machines and spin dryers. Often it had to be all done again and 'mangles' (wound by hand) were used in place of spin dryers. When the anguished cry of 'There've Clorst Mill " went up (purely for selfish reasons) but still pitying the out of work labourers, they were secretly delighted. At last, they could get their washing nice and white. The concern was slowly being generated, largely over public health reasons, and the people in general (although they did not have to tell the miners that) there was a danger also to the environment. Radio programmes appeared such as 'focus on smoke', and when television came on the scene and if the working classes could eventually afford one, the warnings became more intense. The Trade Unions (not before time) began making more noise toward the employers who seemed to keep so distant from it all, were forced to take action, both in regard to working conditions and with regard to their factories emissions.

Clean Air Acts became enforced, car fuel lead content reduced and engine emissions controlled, things where finally looking up. These things actually had positive effects and the result is, that the air we breathe today has never been cleaner than that which our predecessors had to endure.

However, we cannot be complacent, there is still work to be done to ensure we continue to protect our planet some philosophically attuned person once proclaimed that the Earth is comparable to a living thing that strives to take care of itself. It struggles to maintain the correct proportions of gases necessary for its well being, threatened by the 'bacteria' on its surface (A.K.A humans) this bacteria stings and stripes its skin by denuding its forests and ripping out its hair.

The natural telluric currents (or nervous system) that are marred by the scar tissue (we call concrete) all over its body. It may not tolerate such abuse indefinitely.

At this point we could return to the problem (or mystery) of how the Earth maintains its vital percentages of gasses that makeup our atmosphere.

It has been suggested that the balance could be somehow kept in equilibrium by the Oceans that comprise so much surface area of the globe and that the Oceans are the great regulatory engine that keeps everything in balance. We could go further and suggest that the beautiful tiny particles that exist in their billions in the Oceans, that we call 'diatoms' are responsible for absorbing (as well as the trees) any excess carbon that we are all forced to worry about.

When these minute particles are microscopically analysed they display beautiful symmetrical patterns that have inspired the jewellers and their designs. The incredible patterns of these and the snowflakes we magnify, must be the subject of some unknown force of an electro-magnetic nature that may also cause the amazing designs of the crop circles.

Crop circles have been produced by humans in the early more crude designs but they are not a new trendy idea. A woodcut exists of a demonic looking creature actually creating one that was carved in the 1600's it was known as a 'Mowing Devil'.

The amazingly intricate ones have been put under scrutiny and monitored, hoping either to catch possible fraudsters or to explain the cause. Strange lights have been noted passing back and forth over the field. All these oddities, the diatoms, the snowflakes, ball lightning and the crop circles, may well be as said, the results of some so far unexplained electronic force. Perhaps we should give a thought to the farmers who have to put up with all the sightseers and trespassers trampling into their fields to get a better look or scientific teams with special authority to analyse them and so forth. It must cost them financially to straighten everything out.

However, with regard to the causes and the loss of all the trees that where industriously producing all that oxygen, we do not seem to be any the worse for it. We could imagine all the trees in the local woods whispering about it all, in their monthly conference, "Well ….. as the mariner said to the mermaid, we'll just have to make the best of it". Another whispers, "Let's look on the bright side, OK, our numbers are being greatly reduced, it's tough on them but think of all the extra carbon for us after all we all love it and are happy to get a little extra".

All this may not be as imaginative as we may think. Trees are living things just as plants are. There have been some interesting experiments carried out that were designed to analyse and detect the nervous system of the plants, using delicate instruments and probes and electrodes attached to the plants. The plants appeared to react to both mental thoughts and direct verbal tones directed at them.

In one case an attempt was made to detect an emotional response in the plant by directing strong thoughts to the plants, such as, "You are nothing but an ugly weed and I am going to pull you out of the ground and throw you onto the rubbish tip". Amazingly, the plant responds by (not noticeably) trembling that was noted on the instrument readouts, rather like those used to detect Earth tremors or in lie detectors. Fear and nervousness were indicated.

On the other hand, the opposite approach was utilised. Positive and admiring thoughts both mental and verbal where directed at the plant, remarking how beautiful it was and it would certainly produce a fine crop of tomatoes etc. amazingly a much calmer indication appeared on the readout (perhaps the plant was just saying "Thank you very much"). It was also notable that a crop of much more and much larger tomatoes where produced. Naturally, the cynics would reply that may not have observed the results, would immediately judge things differently.

However, having obtained the information they sought what would they do with it? Farmers and nurseries could not be expected to hire teams of people to walk among the tomato plants and the wheat fields remarking how beautiful the growing forms all were.

Only the other day, an item of interest stated that a team of people had been assigned to closely analyse the buzzing of bees and the various intonations and what they mean. All very interesting for some, but another group would say "do we really care?" it is quite amazing just how many tests have been carried out by formulating teams or special study groups to analyse this that or the other issue.

However, the more things we discover the more secrets we will uncover with regard to the living creatures and living life forms of the world. It is all simply a quest for knowledge that drives the human entity and separates us from the other creatures by such a huge margin. It makes the cynics appear so negative. Nevertheless the cynics will always be there and with regard to the aforementioned plant experiments they will take the view that it is not that the plant has fallen in love with you by producing all those big tomatoes because you 'cosied-up to it', but that you simply provided it with more carbon dioxide than the other plants. However, of course, this pragmatic view, although valid in part, does not explain the electronic responses and obvious reaction from the plants.

In any case, a plant's ability to be sensitive to its surroundings, is well supported by other events, for example the strange ability of the 'telegraph vine', is allegedly proven, with its strange power to 'talk' or signal to others of its kind from a great distance away.

We could ask several questions, for example, how does it know where the other plants are? It would have to be given some kind of grid location before commencing the signal. We could also ask what does it have to signal about. one might imagine that it could say "We've heard it on the 'grapevine' that your field is going to be ploughed over", what could the receiving plants do about it? They could not up sticks and move away like the 'triffids' in a science fiction movie.

However, there is no question that plants being a living species do respond to their environment and how they are treated. If we return to this alleged overabundance of carbon, it is more than probable that the trees and plants are more than happy with it. They love it, and as long as we continually supply it, they will happily digest it (but we do not want them to over eat).

Nevertheless, our dangerous attempts to destroy them 'en masse' in the name of progress and development, the Earth still has masses of greenery and oxygen producing growths and the forestry commission are planting large amounts of trees on a daily basis, although perhaps not at the same rate that we cut them down.

The plain fact is that humans have always been as destructive as they are creative. We must never take the dear old Earth for granted, we are still a very long way from terraformed Mars and Venus and start plundering their resources but apart from anything unforeseen, we will eventually do this, and also our Moon along the way. After that it will be the turn of the asteroids and comets.

However, back on Earth, there is one thing we cannot excuse ourselves for it is our careless behaviour with regard to plastics. It is already in the food chain. Some years ago, I can recall a rail trip up Mount Snowden, we chose to walk back down but we were never out of sight of signs of human rubbish wantonly discarded all the way down. Even along the rail track that must have been thrown from the train. The problem is even more noticeable on the average beach towards the end of the day.

Biodegradable processes were known about fifty years ago, one need not ask why industry did not widely adopt it. Almost certainly 'expense' they went for the cheaper option. There are plenty of people alive today who remember the paper shopping bags that were issued. How long did it take us to finally outlaw plastic bags? We have polluted the mountains, the beaches, the seas, but the greatest of all is to pollute our Earth space. It is said that there are some ten thousand pieces of space junk or hardware rattling around our planet at the moment. There is an amazing piece of film taken from the space shuttle. It shows an unknown object in the form of a pinpoint of light in orbit, suddenly there was a flash from below on the Earth, then a streak of light like a laser that shot up toward the object. The object took evasive action and the light streaked through the spot where the object would have been.

If the secretive forces on Earth wish to risk retaliatory action by firing at a non-earthly source, which the object may have been, why not carry out your target practice on the space junk floating around above? Surely, you must be aware of their orbits.

Imagine a headline 'Astronaut killed by astronaut's glove'. These items are travelling at very high speed. In the early days of the space walks from the Mercury and Gemini programmes, every time the hatch was opened something floated out of the capsule with little sign of any attempt to stop it.

Even more serious is our radiated seas and oceans. Radioactivity contaminated flotsam has washed up on the coast of Western Canada that crossed the Pacific after this Fukushima Explosion. How many pacific prawns and salmon are swimming around heavily radiated waiting to go into the nets?

We are told that the ships setting out for the catch must travel out to a distance of around twenty-five miles, but who tells the fish where they should go or where they should swim. If we had not been so quick to get rid of the shuttle fleet surely they could have been utilised to sweep up some of the space junk and lessen the threat of space walking astronauts who have to venture outside at times not to mention the space shuttle itself which sometimes has to manoeuvre out of the way of an object that is threatening it. However, we can take heart from the fact that we have overcome the first hurdle and that is, we 'have' a massive problem to deal with, but we must deal with it. Perhaps we could invoke the old Eastern proverb, "The difference between what we can do and what we cannot do is the measure of man's will". By far the worst aspect of pollution is plastic. Perhaps I should have called this chapter 'My Plastic Footprint'.

END

www.ingramcontent.com/pod-product-compliance
Lightning Source LLC
Chambersburg PA
CBHW020806160426
43192CB00006B/465